Life

at the Top

Life
at the Top

Weather, Wonder & High Cuisine
from the
Mount Washington Observatory

Eric Pinder

HOBBLEBUSH BOOKS
Brookline, New Hampshire

Composed in Arno Pro with Cronos Pro Display at Hobblebush Books

Printed in the United States of America

This edition is a revised and expanded edition of the book *Life at the Top: Tales, Truths and Trusted Recipes from the Mount Washington Observatory*, published by Down East Books in 1997.

All photographs are from the Mount Washington Observatory unless credited otherwise.

Publisher's Cataloging-In-Publication Data
(Prepared by The Donohue Group, Inc.)

Pinder, Eric, 1970-

  Life at the top : weather, wonder and high cuisine from the Mount Washington Observatory / Eric Pinder. — Rev. and exp. ed.

    p. :ill. ; cm.

  Rev. and exp. ed. of: Life at the top : tales, truths, and trusted recipes from the Mount Washington Observatory. Camden, ME : Down East Books, 1997.

    ISBN: 978-0-9801672-6-9

Mount Washington Observatory—Anecdotes. 2. Mount Washington Observatory—Employees—Social life and customs. 3. Washington, Mount (N.H.)—Description and travel. 4. Washington, Mount (N.H.)—Climate. 5. Cookery—New Hampshire—Washington, Mount. 6. Meteorologists—New Hampshire—Washington, Mount—Social life and customs. I. Title.

QC875.U72 M68555 2009

551.69742/1   2009926460

Published by:

HOBBLEBUSH BOOKS

17-A Old Milford Road
Brookline, New Hampshire 03033

www.hobblebush.com

FOR LYNNE

Contents

Part IV · Recipes from the Rockpile

Favorites from the Highest Kitchen in New England   117

Acknowledgments

THE OBSERVATORY'S SUMMIT CREW, PAST and present, deserves a tremendous thank you for making this book a reality. Special thanks are due to Peter Crane for his inexhaustible reservoir of wisdom, patience, and bad jokes; Guy Gosselin for advice and support in starting this project back in 1997; and Sid Hall and Kathy Gregg at Hobblebush Books for bringing the book into the 21st century.

All photographs are from the Mount Washington Observatory, unless otherwise credited. I thank the Observatory for their use.

I'm grateful to Sarah Shor, Tim Ewald, and Barbara Shor for many years of friendship and encouragement. I also want to extend many thanks to Meredith Piotrow and Steve Piotrow (despite their frustrating habit of beating me at Scrabble), Sarah Long, Meg Prentiss, Katie Hess, Ryan Knapp, Brian Clark, Mark Ross-Parent, Susan Ross-Parent, Jennifer Morin, Lynne D. Host Cushman, Norm Michaels, Chris Uggerholt, Cara Rudio, Scot Henley, and the many staff members, Observatory volunteers, and friends who contributed recipes or suggestions. Your help and enthusiasm are what made this book happen.

AFTER THE DEVASTATING SUMMIT
FIRE OF FEBRUARY 2003.

Preface to the Second Edition

MUCH HAS CHANGED SINCE AN earlier edition of *Life at the Top* appeared in bookstores in 1997. New people and a new cat now greet visitors to the Observatory, and they have new stories to tell and breathtaking experiences of their own in the dangerous and exhilarating wind, ice, and fog of Mount Washington.

Newly installed hi-tech scientific instruments help the summit crew monitor some of the worst weather on Earth. Another decade's worth of temperature and snowfall measurements fills the record books, and even the old windchill chart that was prominently displayed on the countertop in the Observatory kitchen is now obsolete. (The National Weather Service revised the official windchill index in 2001.) Elsewhere in New England, the Red Sox finally got around to winning the World Series, and the Patriots switched from perennial losers to occasional champions after changing their decades-old uniform logo.

Speaking of changing uniforms, the current summit crew keeps warm in slick red Observatory jackets and gear donated by L.L.Bean instead of the blue gear of yesteryear. The old handwritten logbooks, kept by weather observers on the summit since 1932, have been largely supplanted by "observer comments" on the Observatory's popular newfangled web site. And it's not like the old days when we had to walk to work eight miles uphill both ways in a blizzard. Well, actually, I suppose that part hasn't changed much, except that the weekly 7.6-mile commute up the Mount Washington Auto Road is now done in a white or yellow Bombardier instead of the old red Sno-Cat.

A devastating fire forever changed the summit architecture in February of 2003. The flames destroyed the TV-8 transmitter building and the summit generators, forcing an evacuation of the suddenly powerless and unheated Observatory for the first time in memory. Meteorologist Sarah Curtis Long describes her first trip back to the summit a year after the fire. "Rounding the bend up the service road, you first notice the Stage Office, and that building was untouched," Sarah says. "Look straight ahead, however, and there was a fresh void—fresh to my eyes anyway. The first thing that struck me was how vulnerable it all is. When I left the summit, that building housed the folks and equipment that kept the summit running; now there was nothing but a concrete pad with a great view."

Mount Monroe, the Lakes of the Clouds, and the southern Presidential Range all slope away toward the horizon just below where the building used to stand. "That thought also went through my head," says Sarah. "I thought, wow, they really had a great view out their kitchen window all those years!"

More memories flooded back as she viewed the scene. "Memories that I shared with Lynne and the guys over at TV," she recalls, "of holiday dinners, afternoon catnaps in the comfortable chairs when I needed to get away for a half-hour."

No one inhabited the building when the fire started. For decades, Marty Engstrom and the TV-8 engineers had shared the summit with the Observatory crew, but TV-8 relocated their transmitter in 2002, several months before the fire. "The summit changed when the transmitter station closed down and the crew made their last shift change," Sarah remembers. Then came the fire. "It seemed the landscape had just caught up with that change in the summit community."

What *hasn't* changed on Mount Washington? The howling winds and the breathtaking scenery are still the same (on the rare occasions that the summit isn't shrouded in fog), and so are the colorful personalities and enthusiasm for wild weather of the handful of people who live and work among the clouds. These are their stories.

Introduction

An Iceberg in the Sky

WHO WOULD HAVE GUESSED THAT the windiest, most wintry weather in the world occurs not in the Himalayas or on the icy tundra of Antarctica, but right here in the hills and mountains of New England?

On Mount Washington, highest peak in the Presidential Range of New Hampshire, blizzards regularly pummel the summit, sometimes even in summer. Bone-numbing cold, frequent fog, and furious winds have earned this lofty peak a nickname: "Home of the World's Worst Weather."

This is a book about Mount Washington and its savage skies and the unusual lives of the handful of people who eat, sleep, work, and play in a land above the clouds.

Mount Washington is a 400-million-year-old spike of metamorphic rock thrusting high above the hills of New Hampshire. Expansive views of sparkling blue lakes and rolling hills entice thousands of sightseers to climb up the slopes to its 6,288-foot summit each summer. They visit when the temperature and wind are relatively mild: Gentle breezes caress the brows of weary hikers like a cool, damp cloth. But in winter, the wind turns formidable—sometimes deadly. Whenever I strap on my winter hiking boots and scramble up a high ridge on the mountain, I brace against the nearly constant wind. Gusts scissor through my jacket and hurl chunks of ice the size of cinder blocks into the sky. My nose reddens, and I fight back a sneeze. A powerful gust knocks me sideways, like a punch delivered by a strong invisible hand.

At any time of year, the mountain may be swept by winds so strong they can hoist me into the sky like a kite. Rather than walk, I must fly down the trail; the flaps of my jacket flutter against my ribs like wings. I wobble to keep my balance and try to walk in a straight line. All across the summit cone, I see other hikers buffeted by wind. They walk in jerky, mechanical steps through the gusts, like marionettes with missing strings.

Despite these extreme conditions—or, more accurately, because of them—Mount Washington is home to a small crew of scientists who live and work on the windy summit, keeping track of the notorious weather.

The Mount Washington Observatory was established as a private nonprofit organization in 1932 to study weather and climate trends. The Observatory's wintry conditions attract scientists and researchers who are studying cold-weather climates. "We're really an arctic island in a temperate zone," explains staff meteorologist Mark Ross-Parent. "There's something about weather extremes that people love."

A healthy sense of humor helps the staff to take demanding conditions in stride. Mark boasts that he has "the highest paying job in New England." Unfortunately, that refers to his elevation, not his wages. "Working here really limits your upward mobility," another meteorologist quips.

Two crews work on the summit on alternate weeks, and their duties include scientific research, weather reporting, daily radio broadcasts— and, of course, shoveling snow: "Wow! Two days in a row of strange white stuff. I think it could be snow, but there's so darn much of it, I can't really be sure," writes one scientist in the Observatory logbook on a January day. A little later he adds: "The sledding should be fairly decent tomorrow. The crew (all two of us) spent the day shoveling, but it seems to be blowing right back in, so that all evidence of our hard work will be gone by tomorrow. Memo to the other shift: We really did shovel. Really! Trust us."

Life at the Top takes a look at life on the summit, where workdays are punctuated by visits from wild foxes and soaring ravens. In daylight, we catch glimpses of flying saucer-shaped lenticular clouds in orbit around the peaks. Clear nights sometimes bring spectacular views of meteor showers or the aurora borealis. Swirling snow wraps around us like a blindfold in winter, forcing us to retreat indoors. And at dinnertime, the aroma of spicy spinach quiche wafts up from the kitchen.

Quiche? Would you believe that people who are crazy enough to sled down the six-thousand-foot-high mountain in the raw grip of January can also be gourmet cooks? Workers on Mount Washington endure the worst blows of winter weather, but they compensate by eating well—and often—so any book about the Observatory crew's trials and triumphs naturally must include a selection of favorite recipes. You'll find them beginning on page 117.

"If you don't like the weather, wait a minute," is an old Yankee aphorism. On Mount Washington, they say it with a twist: "If you don't like the weather, go someplace else!" But have a bite to eat before you go.

LENTICULAR CLOUDS HOVER OVER MT. WASHINGTON WHILE CUMULUS CLOUDS WHISK BY IN THE WIND.

Part I

Summit Science

Chapter 1

The Story in the Stones— Mount Washington's Geology

DURING SHIFT CHANGE AT THE Observatory, the roof of the Bombardier snow tractor is piled high with boxes of fresh food, supplies, books, new research equipment, and backpacks from the crew stuffed with a week's worth of clothes. The first chore upon arriving at the summit is to unload all those heavy packs and boxes, brush off the snow, and carry them inside. You'll often hear the familiar question, "What have you got in here, *rocks?*"

You're a geologist if your answer to that question has ever been "Yes!" According to an old joke, if you're a geologist, all the baggage handlers at the airport know you by name and refuse to help with your luggage.

Geology is the study of rocks. It's a hard (pardon the pun) subject. Enthusiastic geology students like to say, "Geology rocks!" And there are plenty of rocks of interest to geologists here on Mount Washington.

For obvious reasons, Mount Washington is called the "Rockpile" by the hardy souls who live and work on its windy summit. Jagged boulders jut through the clouds, and stones tumble down the trails, kicked loose by hikers' boots. Steep ravines and rocky ridges cut across the skyline thousands of feet above timberline. But where did this jumble of stones come from? To read the clues in the rocks themselves, we must climb to the summit, close our eyes, and strain to imagine the events of the distant past. Only in our minds can we witness the tumultuous evolution of Mount Washington.

The Evolution of Rocks

Surprisingly, in our search for the origins of the highest peak in New England, we must first look far beneath the sea.

The stones that sit today on the summit of Mount Washington were born during the Paleozoic Era, some 400 million years ago, when layers of sand and mud were deposited in shallow seas and compressed into sedimentary rock in a swampy region near Earth's equator. Over the course of many millions of years, these shallow waters disappeared as our continent drifted north into colder climates.

Three hundred million years ago, the continents of Europe and Africa rubbed against the coast of North America, squeezing out the ocean in between. As a result of this collision, miles of sedimentary rock were crumpled deep inside Earth's mantle. Sandstones and shales that had long ago formed in New England's ancient seas were slowly metamorphosed by intense heat and pressure. Metamorphic rocks known as schist,

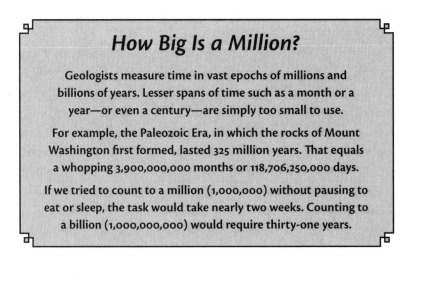

How Big Is a Million?

Geologists measure time in vast epochs of millions and billions of years. Lesser spans of time such as a month or a year—or even a century—are simply too small to use.

For example, the Paleozoic Era, in which the rocks of Mount Washington first formed, lasted 325 million years. That equals a whopping 3,900,000,000 months or 118,706,250,000 days.

If we tried to count to a million (1,000,000) without pausing to eat or sleep, the task would take nearly two weeks. Counting to a billion (1,000,000,000) would require thirty-one years.

ON THE ROCKS WITH NIN.

gneiss, and quartzite were the result. Today, these rocks sit atop Mount Washington.

Why do the rocks sparkle? On rare days when the sun actually peeks through the clouds, boulders on Mount Washington's summit glitter and gleam. Each stone is studded with tiny mirrorlike plates of mica, a soft, easily scratched mineral that forms in paper-thin sheets. Mica is created when sedimentary rocks such as sandstone or shale are metamorphosed deep below Earth's surface. The mineral is one clue that helps geologists unlock the mysteries of Mount Washington's past.

By looking at the texture and mineral content of rocks, geologists can determine the temperature and pressure at which these rocks formed. In the case of Mount Washington, sedimentary rocks made of clay, sand, and mud were at one time squeezed and heated several miles underground. The pressure at these depths was six kilobars, six thousand times stronger than the pressure at Earth's surface. That's enough to instantly flatten a pickup truck into a tiny sliver of steel. The temperature in this geological pressure cooker was 1,100°F, a far cry from the annual average of 26.5°F that the rocks of the summit experience today.

Why are the rocks wavy or bent? High temperatures and pressures tend to make rock elastic. Just as metal bends and ruptures during a car crash, the bedrock was "crumpled" by the impact of Europe and Africa against the coast of North America roughly 300 million years ago.

Was Mount Washington once a volcano? New Hampshire is known as the Granite State, but granite is extremely rare on Mount Washington. Granite is a rock formed from magma. Geologists once believed that no granite (nor any other igneous or volcanic material) existed on Mount Washington. You can find granitic material on the slopes, just not very much. The primary bedrock in the Presidential Range is mica schist, a metamorphic rock. Mount Washington was never a volcano. (Well, except for the time a crew member cooked Nuclear Rice & Beans in the Observatory kitchen. See page 165.)

Are there any fossils on the mountain? Some of the State Park crew have been there so long and are so set in their ways that they're jokingly described as "old fossils." But no real fossils have been discovered on Mount Washington, though fossils from the Mesozoic Era exist elsewhere in New England, particularly in the Connecticut River Valley. The clay, sandstone, and mudstone that first formed the rocks of Mount Washington predate all but the earliest life on Earth. Whatever earlier fossils once existed in those ancient rocks were probably "cooked" away by intense heat and pressure when the original sedimentary rocks were metamorphosed into today's schist, quartzite, and gneiss. (*Gneiss* is pronounced "nice," which leads geologists to joke about "nice rocks." In earthquake-prone areas—near fault lines—some geologists have been known to stand amid the wreckage and quip, "It's not my fault!")

Sawdust from the Log
June 16, 1995

"I think Mount Washington is going to erupt!
Actually, we experienced a mild earthquake early
this morning. We heard the floor rumble, but most
of the crew slept right through it."

A Tour through Time

The Rockpile has passed through millions of years of heat and cold, rain and drought, upheaval and decay. Mount Washington's summit, currently the highest point of land in New England, long ago lay at the bottom of the sea. What geological events brought about this change? To get to the roots of Mount Washington's history, we must first delve deep into the past.

Our imaginary trip through time begins more than 500 million years ago, in the early Paleozoic Era. So pack a lunch and fasten your seatbelt, because we're in for a long, bumpy ride. Mount Washington does not yet exist. In fact, no solid ground at all exists in the region that will one day be known as New Hampshire. Our time machine splashes down in a warm Paleozoic sea. Soon we must wade waist-deep through shallow waters. I hope you brought some waterproof boots. A tropical sun glares down at us, and tiny eyeless animals called trilobites scurry in the mud and sand at our feet.

Let's fast-forward through the next 10 million years. Layers of sand and mud thicken and harden into stone. (Far, far in the future, these rocks and others like them will rise from the sea to a height of 6,288 feet, forming the jagged tip of Mount Washington.)

Another ten million years spin by in the blink of an eye. Staring down into murky pools of water, we see the faces of trilobites sprout eyes. Distant continents lurch from the tropics and creep north, inch by inch. If we gaze at this faraway land through a telescope, we see nothing but stark, naked rock, not clothed by plants or trees. Not a single blade of grass waves in the wind. Why, it's so long ago, politicians running for president haven't even started campaigning there yet!

Again, millions of years pass by. In time, the blue outlines of Europe and Africa appear on the horizon. The two continents swim closer year by year. The ocean starts to close.

Deep beneath the surface of the waves, the continental plates of North America, Europe, and Africa nudge together. A string of island volcanoes erupts and spews fire into the water.

The time is now 350 million years ago. The first primitive trees start to clothe the land; a stubble of needles and cones covers the rolling plains. In the seas, the trilobites have long since become extinct, and their fossils are empty shells, death masks embedded in the rocks.

Out on the ocean, volcanic islands slowly sink into the sea, a process that takes millions of years. The ocean continues to close. As the Old World collides with the New, rocks made from hardened lava smash against the coastline of North America. During the impact, the sedimentary rocks we have been standing on are thrust deep underground, where they are squeezed and folded. In the depths of Earth, heat and pressure melt the ancient sedimentary rocks at our feet, cooking a stew of mica and quartz. For an eon, these rocks and minerals—and our imaginary time capsule—are buried miles below the surface, boiling at 1,100°F. But at long last, the mica schist bedrock of Mount Washington is created.

Soon the proto-Atlantic Ocean is gone. In its place, the continents of Europe, Africa, and North America are firmly welded together into one supercontinent. We have arrived at the start of the Mesozoic Era, the Age of Reptiles, 245 million years ago.

The impact of the Old World against the coast of North America has thrust up a mountain range as high as today's Rockies. While we watch, the blur of a million seasons wears the mountains down.

Tiny reptiles dash and dart among the rocks, the earliest reptilian ancestors of dinosaurs. The time is 240 million years in the past. From a window in our time capsule, we see a crack appear between the Americas and the Old World. At long last, the Atlantic Ocean is born, a sliver of blue water splitting the world in two.

The early Appalachian Mountains continue to erode for millions of years. Soil and minerals wash down streams into the newborn sea. As the mountains shrink, a great weight is lifted from the shoulders of the land; the ground rises. Somewhere far below the soil, a rock that will one day sit atop Mount Washington inches toward the surface.

During the next 200 million years, the shadow of Europe pulls away across a widening Atlantic Ocean. The tiny lizards evolve into dinosaurs and flourish. (Be careful if you wander away from our time machine. Look at the teeth on that T-Rex!) Little do the dinosaurs realize that they will soon follow the trilobites into the oblivion of extinction.

A ROCKY RIDE TO THE SUMMIT IN THE BOMBARDIER.

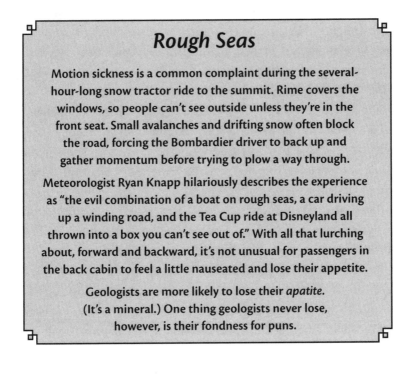

Rough Seas

Motion sickness is a common complaint during the several-hour-long snow tractor ride to the summit. Rime covers the windows, so people can't see outside unless they're in the front seat. Small avalanches and drifting snow often block the road, forcing the Bombardier driver to back up and gather momentum before trying to plow a way through.

Meteorologist Ryan Knapp hilariously describes the experience as "the evil combination of a boat on rough seas, a car driving up a winding road, and the Tea Cup ride at Disneyland all thrown into a box you can't see out of." With all that lurching about, forward and backward, it's not unusual for passengers in the back cabin to feel a little nauseated and lose their appetite.

Geologists are more likely to lose their *apatite*. (It's a mineral.) One thing geologists never lose, however, is their fondness for puns.

The time is now 70 million years ago. From the safety of our time capsule, we watch a comet or meteorite streak through the atmosphere and explode off the coast of Mexico. Its impact rattles Earth, spewing millions of tons of dust into the sky and blocking the warm rays of the sun. Volcanoes erupt and clog the sky with even more dust and ash. As plants wither and die, starving animals stagger across the land in search of food. During the chill years that follow, nearly 75 percent of all life on Earth vanishes—including the last of the dinosaurs.

When the dust finally clears, surviving species crawl out of the shadows. Earth is reborn. Plants burst into flower, and hundreds of species of grasses roll across the plains, waving like banners in the wind.

But what about Mount Washington? After millions of years of erosion and uplift, the tip of New England's highest peak finally pokes through to the surface. The mountain is later chipped and hewed by wind, rain, and ice, until at last it resembles the familiar cone-shaped mountain we know today. Much of the fine sculpture-work on Mount Washington occurred during the ice ages of the last two million years.

If we travel in our time capsule to the Pleistocene Epoch, we can watch a tongue of ice ooze down from the northern tundra, flattening forests and scraping away the soil. Gradually, an enormous ice sheet nudges against the base of Mount Washington. It sweeps around the mountain to the south, dipping its icy paws into the sea.

Thousands of years pass, and the ice layer thickens. Mount Jefferson and the rest of the northern Presidential Range soon succumb to the ice and disappear beneath it. Mount Washington appears as a snowy mound, protruding just a few hundred feet above the ice. Soon, it too is buried by the glacier.

The time is now 20,000 years in the past. The glacier scrapes across the mountain and carves a pair of basins in the rock. Later these basins fill with water. Today, we call them Lakes of the Clouds.

Ten thousand years pass, and the climate warms. The continental ice sheet slowly melts away until the land we know as New England is mostly free of ice, exposed to the sun. It is an ugly rubble-heap of broken rock, stripped of soils and trees. On Mount Washington, small valley glaciers—chunks of ice as large as small hills—linger on the slopes. Gradually, these tiny glaciers pry open chasms called cirques, like Tuckerman Ravine and the Great Gulf.

The time is now 6,000 years ago, and the valley glaciers have dwindled. Only a small hillock of snow snuggled in Tuckerman Ravine remains. For six thousand winters, right up to the present day, frost seeps into nooks and niches on Mount Washington. House-sized boulders split and crumble, pulled apart by fingers of ice. Avalanches of lichen-covered boulders thunder down the slopes, landing in piles of rubble in the basins. As soil and plants return to New England, a softwood forest creeps up the mountain's lower slopes.

Finally, after a journey of 500 million years, our time capsule returns us to the Rockpile as it is today, i.e., crowded with sightseers on the summit. Thank you for joining us on this tour through time. Don't forget to sign the guestbook or buy a postcard and a T-shirt at the summit gift shop.

What Makes a Glacier

At the height of the last ice age, a glacier scraped across the mountain, scattering stones and boulders from distant lands (glacial erratics) on the slopes. ("But where is the glacier now?" a curious visitor to the summit once asked a North Country native. Replied that crusty old New England Yankee, "Ma'am, it's gone back for another load!") Although frost action accounts for most of the broken boulders we see above timberline, glacial ice has certainly left its signature on the summit. Mount Washington is like a work of art, a statue more than 400 million years in the making. Glaciers were the chisels that applied the final touches.

Where did the glaciers come from? At the start of the Pleistocene Era, roughly two million years ago, climatic instabilities produced worldwide fluctuations in temperature. Four ice ages, each lasting tens of thousands of years, occurred in the Pleistocene. During each one, vast sheets of ice spread across much of North America, burying New England's mountains, including Mount Washington.

A HIKER ADMIRES A GLACIER-SCULPTED LANDSCAPE.

Before the last ice age, Mount Washington was a taller and rounder mountain, much like those of the Great Smokies today. The Great Gulf, Tuckerman Ravine, and other steep, jagged cliffs that plunge down the mountainside are relatively new features, sculpted by glaciers.

At its peak, the ice sheet was more than a mile thick, a weight so heavy that the land beneath it sank. Every land mass on Earth "floats" on a layer of hot, liquid magma (molten lava deep underground), which gives it a special kind of buoyancy. If a cement block is placed on the deck of a tiny sailboat, the boat's hull sinks lower in the water. Similarly, a great weight like an ice cap—or a mountain range—tends to press down on the land around it. When the ice cap melts or the mountains erode, the burden becomes lighter and the landscape rebounds.

The New England landscape has risen and fallen many times during the past 500 million years. As recently as fifteen thousand years ago, the weight of a continental ice cap pressed down on the New England land-scape like a firm hand. Later, when the glaciers melted and the weight disappeared, the land recoiled like an ancient, rusty spring. Glacial erratics—rocks carried to the mountain from distant locations—are proof that an ice sheet once covered Mount Washington.

Sculpted by Ice

Many features shaped by glaciation are visible from the summit, the Mount Washington Auto Road, or the hiking trails.

Cirques are giant U-shaped valleys gouged out of the mountainside by valley glaciers. The last of these small glaciers melted away more than six thousand years ago, long after the continental ice sheet had retreated. Tuckerman Ravine and the Great Gulf are both cirques.

Tarns are basins scraped into the rocks by the motion of ice as glaciers slid across the land. The ice age potholes later filled with water, forming high-altitude ponds such as the Lakes of the Clouds. These lakes, hud-dled below the north slope of Mount Monroe, are the highest freshwater ponds in the Northeast. They are easily viewed from the flat rocks south of the site of the old TV building on the summit of Mount Washington.

MOUNT MONROE OVERLOOKS THE LAKES OF
THE CLOUDS HUT AND GLACIAL TARNS.

Roches moutonées. As the great ice sheet spread across North America, it scooped up stones, gravel, and boulders and carried them south. Like a continent-sized piece of sandpaper, the glacier and its load of debris scraped across the mountains, sanding smooth the northerly slopes and "plucking off" the southern edges. Many rocky outcroppings in New England possess a long, gently sloping north side with a nearly vertical drop to the south. They are called sheepbacks, whalebacks, or *roches moutonées.* Mount Monroe is a giant sheepback, with a gentle slope in the northwest (the direction of the advancing glacier) and a jagged cliff in the southeast.

Glacial striations. A glance at many of the boulders above treeline reveals pale white lines running in a northwest-to-southeast direction. These are scars left behind by the continental ice sheet.

After the Glaciers' Retreat

When the Wisconsin Ice Age ended, approximately eight thousand years ago, the newly exposed landscape looked like a subarctic tundra. Ice had stripped away trees, grasses, and soil, and most animals had fled south in search of warmer climates. Gradually, however, spruces, firs, and other trees returned, and with them came the animal species that continue to inhabit the New England woods today.

As the climate warmed, hundreds of arctic plants and animals that had moved into New England during the last ice age could no longer survive—except on windy peaks above treeline, where the climate was still subarctic. Flowers such as *Diapensia lapponica* and Lapland rosebay are alpine refugees, stranded above treeline on Mount Washington and a few other high peaks in the Northeast.

HIKERS HAVE ENJOYED THE VIEWS ABOVE
THE GREAT GULF SINCE DARBY FIELD FIRST
ASCENDED MT. WASHINGTON IN 1642.

THIS FAMOUS SIGN MARKS THE PLACE WHERE HISTORY WAS MADE.

Chapter 2

The World's Worst Weather—And What Causes It

YOU'VE PROBABLY HEARD THE OLD expression, "March comes in like a lion and goes out like a lamb." How about, "A cold May is good for corn and hay"? Both of these tidbits of weather wisdom originated as folklore hundreds of years ago and were passed down from generation to generation.

Weather folklore played a crucial role in the lives of our ancestors. For farmers in New England, especially, failure to keep a close eye on the weather led to poor harvests and widespread famine. "Make hay while the sun shines" was a particularly popular piece of weather folklore. The only problem was, our ancestors had no way of knowing for certain whether the sun *would* shine. They couldn't rely on satellite images or watch a snappily dressed TV meteorologist give a forecast on the evening news. Instead, they looked to the only weather forecaster available: Mother Nature.

The natural world is full of clues about weather. For example, consider the old saying, "As the days lengthen, so the cold strengthens." During the icy blue days of January and February, before spring rains washed away winter, people in New England huddled by their fires to keep warm, but they still had hope for the coming harvest season: "If February gives much snow, a fine summer it doth foreshow."

Unfortunately, weather has always been a fickle creature, and even the most popular folklore sayings sometimes get it wrong. Despite a wealth of weather wisdom, our ancestors were still caught by surprise by sudden storms or killing frosts. "Never trust a July sky," they vowed.

Even today, here in New England, we grudgingly acknowledge the fickle nature of weather. "If you don't like the weather here . . . " You know the rest. Apparently, the only unchanging thing about weather is that it *always* changes.

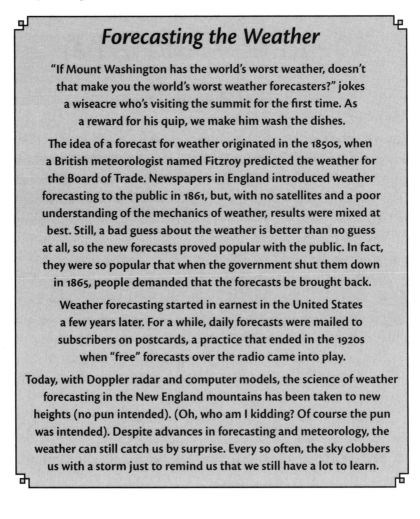

Forecasting the Weather

"If Mount Washington has the world's worst weather, doesn't that make you the world's worst weather forecasters?" jokes a wiseacre who's visiting the summit for the first time. As a reward for his quip, we make him wash the dishes.

The idea of a forecast for weather originated in the 1850s, when a British meteorologist named Fitzroy predicted the weather for the Board of Trade. Newspapers in England introduced weather forecasting to the public in 1861, but, with no satellites and a poor understanding of the mechanics of weather, results were mixed at best. Still, a bad guess about the weather is better than no guess at all, so the new forecasts proved popular with the public. In fact, they were so popular that when the government shut them down in 1865, people demanded that the forecasts be brought back.

Weather forecasting started in earnest in the United States a few years later. For a while, daily forecasts were mailed to subscribers on postcards, a practice that ended in the 1920s when "free" forecasts over the radio came into play.

Today, with Doppler radar and computer models, the science of weather forecasting in the New England mountains has been taken to new heights (no pun intended). (Oh, who am I kidding? Of course the pun was intended). Despite advances in forecasting and meteorology, the weather can still catch us by surprise. Every so often, the sky clobbers us with a storm just to remind us that we still have a lot to learn.

Wind

Mount Washington's infamous weather reputation is mostly due to its winds. All year long, rivers of wind cascade across the cold stones and slither down the slopes. The wind refuses to stop, even when the air turns warm and the storms of winter wither in the sun. In fact, spring is the season when Mount Washington first entered the

BRACING AGAINST THE WIND.

record books for wild weather. Mount Washington's reputation for fierce winds was firmly cemented on the stormy afternoon of April 12, 1934, when a gust howled across the summit at 231 mph. No stronger wind has ever been measured on Earth's surface.

That doesn't mean no stronger winds have ever occurred. They just haven't been accurately measured (at least not on the surface). Any stronger wind tends to destroy the anemometer that's trying to measure it.

The official record refers to *surface* wind speed. "What about tornadoes?" people often ask. Winds topping 300 mph certainly rage in the twisting funnels of the most powerful tornadoes. But the Doppler radar tracking those winds is measuring the speed several hundred feet off the ground. And estimates of wind speed based on structural damage are just that—estimates. For that reason alone, Mount Washington's record still stands.

There was no Doppler radar in 1934, and no satellite imagery to warn people that a massive low-pressure system was lurching toward the White Mountains.

History calls it the "Big Wind." In 1934, that record-breaking (and window-breaking) blast of icy air was closely monitored by meteorologists at the Mount Washington Observatory. In fact, the fury of the wind was less remarkable than the fact that humans witnessed the brunt of that storm and lived to tell the tale.

To instill confidence in the Observatory crew during savage storms—or at least to allay their fears of being scooped up and dashed against the rocks—the rickety wooden Observatory building was strapped and buckled to the summit by heavy chains draped across the roof. But on the day of the Big Wind, the chains had not yet been put to the test. No one knew what was coming.

On the morning of April 12, the youngest member of the crew, a twenty-six-year-old engineer named Wendell Stephenson, walked outside to de-ice the instruments with a hammer. Ice had crusted over the anemometer and the wind vanes, resulting in poor readings.

As soon as he stepped out the door, Stephenson's ears were plugged by the roar of the wind; he couldn't hear his own voice even if he screamed.

THE ORIGINAL 1932 OBSERVATORY CREW: ALEX
MCKENZIE, BOB MONAHAN, JOE DODGE, SAL
PAGLIUCA, AND TIKKY THE CAT (IN SAL'S ARM).

Wind thundered against the rocks like giant kettledrums and howled like wolves. (If you were being knocked around by a hurricane-force wind, you'd start mixing your metaphors, too.)

Stephenson climbed the ladder to the tower, but a 160-mile-per-hour gust raced out of the southeast and pinned him to the wall. He could not climb up—or fall down. "If I'd known how strong the wind was, I'd never have gone out there," he said afterward. As it was, he barely managed to crawl back inside.

A few hours later, when the storm raged to even greater intensity, the crew watched the walls of their little wooden shack bulge inward; each strong gust pounded the walls like a giant mallet. Would the building stay put? Or would the wind rip open the walls and fling them off the summit?

Chief Observer Sal Pagliuca climbed outside to de-ice the instruments again. In the logbook he wrote: "I hammered with all my strength, but I doubt the strength of Polyphemus could move a sledgehammer in a 200-miles-per-hour breeze."

Meanwhile, downstairs, using a stopwatch and timing the click of their anemometer, the crew calculated a record wind speed of 231 miles per hour. "Our first thought was, will they believe it?" they wrote in the logbook later that night.

Fortunately, the anemometer and stopwatch were tested and proved true. (The Observatory's Number 2 Heated Anemometer had been tested and calibrated in two National Bureau of Standards wind tunnels in 1933.) A new wind speed was added to the record books. It remains unbroken to this day.

One challenge to Mount Washington's claim to the world's worst weather came in December 17, 1997, when Typhoon Paka slammed against the coast of Guam. Andersen Air Force Base reported a gust of 205 knots, or 236 mph—5 mph faster than Mount Washington's world record gust from 1934! If accurate, the measurement in Guam would be the new record.

The initial reaction at the Observatory was curiosity mixed with a little panic. "What are we going to do with all those T-shirts now?" fretted one Observatory crew member, thinking of all the "231-mph world-record wind" shirts and paraphernalia for sale in the Mount Washington Museum gift shop. We joked about changing our motto: "Home of What Used to Be the World's Worst Weather—that's a bit wordy for a T-shirt, isn't it?" Newspaper and TV journalists started calling the Observatory to see how we felt about "losing our record."

Over the next few days, doubts arose about the accuracy of the 236-mph Guam measurement. "None of our forecasters think it was that high, and we've been unable to confirm it," said Delores Clark of the National Weather Service Pacific Region Office in Hawaii. A NWS team started to analyze the wind data.

"Wait! Don't get rid of all those T-shirts just yet!" someone quipped on the summit. The entire Observatory crew waited in suspense.

In the end, the report of a 236-mph gust was discounted. Andersen Air Force Base used a FMQ-13 hot-wire anemometer, not considered accurate above 150 knots. Power surges and error codes at the time of the measurement cast even more doubt on its accuracy. After two months of investigating Doppler radar, satellite images, denuded trees, damaged buildings, and all the raw data, meteorologists concluded that Typhoon Paka had had gusts up to 173 mph.

For now, Mount Washington's record gust remains unchallenged. For foul-weather fans, a quick glance at wind statistics throughout the year highlights the mountain's appeal:

	Average wind speed (mph)	Highest gust recorded	Direction
January	46.3	173 (1985)	NW
February	44.5	166 (1972)	E
March	41.6	180 (1942)	W
April	36.1	213 (1934)	SE
May	29.7	164 (1945)	W
June	27.7	136 (1949)	NW
July	25.3	154 (1996)	W
August	25.1	142 (1954)	ENE

	Average wind speed (mph)	Highest gust recorded	Direction
September	29.1	174 (1979)	SE
October	33.8	161 (1943)	W
November	39.7	163 (1983)	NW
December	44.8	178 (1980)	NW

It pays to remember that the force of the wind is not the same as its speed. The force of wind increases geometrically. A 50-mile-per-hour gust is not simply twice as strong as a 25-mile-per-hour wind—it's four times as strong!

What makes wind blow? Air molecules flow from areas of high pressure to areas of low pressure. It seems hard to believe, since we are so used to it, but an average of 14.7 pounds of air (per square inch) presses down on our shoulders every second of our lives. Try lifting a 15-pound weight next time you pass the sports section of the local department store, and then consider that that is not too much more than what's pushing against every inch of our skin every day.

We don't notice them, but even on a calm day, individual air molecules are swirling and zigzagging all around us, bumping into each other at incredible speeds that can top 1,000 mph. The impact of all these billions of molecules exerts pressure in all directions, including sideways and upward. The more air molecules there are (and the faster they travel), the higher the pressure. Climb a mountain where the air is thinner, and the pressure goes down. On Mount Washington, at 6,288 feet above sea level, we feel a pressure of only 11.7 pounds per square inch. And on Mount Everest, the tallest mountain in the world at 29,028 feet, only about five pounds per square inch of air settles on each weary climber's shoulders.

Mount Everest stands near the top of the troposphere, the breathable lower layer of our atmosphere. The weight of hundreds of miles of air—most of it too thin to breathe—presses down on the troposphere and holds it close to Earth's surface. Most of the clouds, wind, and

storms we think of as weather occur only in the bottom seven miles of
the atmosphere.

The layer above the troposphere is the stratosphere (where the ozone
layer is), followed by the mesosphere, thermosphere, and exosphere. You
can remember the order of the layers of the atmosphere (starting from
the bottom) with this catchy phrase:

The Sky Makes Things Exciting.

Of course, this leaves out the ionopshere, which overlaps some of the
other layers. So maybe it should be, "The Sky Makes Things Exciting
Indeed." When I mentioned this mnemonic device in an introductory
weather class I was teaching, one student suggested an alternative: Take
Some More Time, Eric.

Oddly enough, no one thought much about the atmosphere until
just a few centuries ago. When an ancient Greek scientist named Hero
first suggested that air was a substance and had weight, he was laughed at.
The idea that atmospheric pressure could be used to predict storms didn't
appear until the seventeenth century, when Italian physicist Evangelista
Torricelli invented the barometer.

NIN INSPECTS THE BAROMETER CASE.

To picture how wind flows, imagine a crowd of people jammed into an elevator, standing so close together that their elbows jostle. As soon as the door opens, they rush outside, where they have more space. Air molecules behave the same way; they flow from high pressure to low pressure, essentially looking for elbow room.

Wind is air running "downhill" from high to low pressure, spreading out as it goes. The greater the difference in pressure between two regions, the faster the wind blows.

Look closely at a weather map next time you watch the forecast. If an H, or high pressure system, sits close to a big L, or low pressure area, you know that a strong wind is on the way. Winds grow stronger and faster when high and low pressure systems move close together.

Since water vapor suspended in the form of clouds makes the atmospheric pressure drop, a dip in the barometer often means a storm is coming. So if you hear the words "rapidly falling barometer" in the forecast, it's time to break out the umbrella. (Well, either that or someone's throwing barometers off the roof.)

Why is Mount Washington so windy? By a strange coincidence, Mount Washington sits at the crossroads of several major storm tracks, including the Atlantic Coast and the line of the Great Lakes. Air masses scoop up moisture from these large bodies of water, forming storm clouds that later wring themselves dry over the hills of New England. Storms also follow the path of the jet stream, a high altitude river of wind. The jet stream veers to the north in the winter and to the south in the summer but on average passes right over New England.

Another source of wind on Mount Washington is a process called the Bernoulli effect. The mountain "squeezes" wind between the summit and a "lid" in the atmosphere called the tropopause. If you have ever stuck your thumb over the end of a garden hose, you know that constricting the opening makes the water shoot faster. Mount Washington has the same effect—the peak juts above the valley like a giant thumb and makes the wind roar.

If you wonder what it feels like to try to stand upright in a hurricane-force wind, just ask the folks at the Observatory. Videotape there offers hours of entertainment, showing people blowing like tumbleweeds across the observation deck. One tape shows a meteorologist slapped away from the door by an invisible paw of wind. To get back, he inches forward but makes no headway. For twenty minutes, he flounders on the deck and gets nowhere, like a salmon trying to swim up a waterfall. Someone jokes: "And we never saw Pete again." On camera, the man shrinks into a ball and spins off the screen, lost in fog.

"I was picked up and thrown across the deck like a human hovercraft," Pete said later. To stop his tumble across the summit, he dragged his hands on the ground for a hundred feet—and ruined a good pair of gloves in the process.

Observers at a U.S. Army Signal Service station on top of Mount Washington in the late 1800s struggled to work in the same hurricane-force winds that the Observatory crew does today. The Signal Service logbook entries tended to be briefer and more formal than today's Observer Comments, but the wind could jolt even them into scribbling down a burst of descriptive prose. After a Sergeant Beals climbed up on the roof to change the anemometer on December 28, 1883, the logbook said, "The reception he met from the raging elements was grievous to relate. A screwdriver was wrenched from his hand, his scarf torn from about his head, and one of his overshoes, which was unbuckled, blown off and carried out of sight over the valley."

I survived a similar ordeal more than a century later. The wind surged, and a loose piece of equipment on the observation deck needed to be lashed down quickly before the gusts yanked it free. So I rushed out with a quick, temporary fix: a roll of duct tape. Somehow the 140-mph winds reached under the hood of my jacket and ripped away my face mask. "There goes forty dollars," I thought, watching the black face mask fly over the railing out of sight. I couldn't unroll the duct tape with gloved hands, so I tried tucking one glove under my shoulder. Whoosh! Away it went. To add insult to injury, the wind tugged the duct tape right out my hand and hurled it down toward Tuckerman Ravine. I imagined the faces of bewildered hikers far down the trail, looking up as first a face mask, then a glove, then a roll of duct tape dropped inexplicably from the heavens.

"What's going on up there!?" they must have wondered. Then I crawled back, embarrassed, to the tower door.

Walking—or even crawling—against hurricane-force winds is so difficult because the force of the wind increases geometrically. For example, a Class 1 hurricane (winds of 74 miles per hour or greater) is strong enough to rip up a small tree like a weed and toss its trunk through a roof. A Class 5 hurricane (above 150 miles per hour) isn't simply twice as strong, it's four times as strong! Imagine trying to stand up while Niagara Falls pours down on your back, and you'll get some idea of the true power of wind. How Sal Pagliuca managed to hold on to a ladder and climb up to the roof in the world record 231-mph wind, we'll never know.

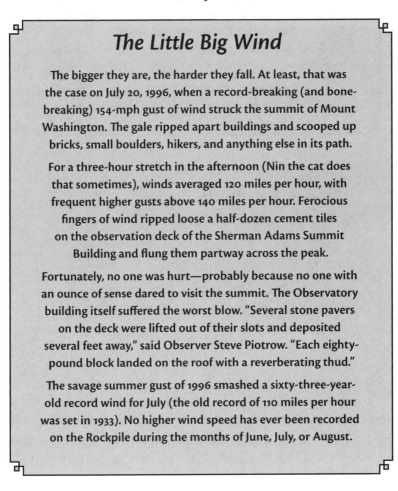

The Little Big Wind

The bigger they are, the harder they fall. At least, that was the case on July 20, 1996, when a record-breaking (and bone-breaking) 154-mph gust of wind struck the summit of Mount Washington. The gale ripped apart buildings and scooped up bricks, small boulders, hikers, and anything else in its path.

For a three-hour stretch in the afternoon (Nin the cat does that sometimes), winds averaged 120 miles per hour, with frequent higher gusts above 140 miles per hour. Ferocious fingers of wind ripped loose a half-dozen cement tiles on the observation deck of the Sherman Adams Summit Building and flung them partway across the peak.

Fortunately, no one was hurt—probably because no one with an ounce of sense dared to visit the summit. The Observatory building itself suffered the worst blow. "Several stone pavers on the deck were lifted out of their slots and deposited several feet away," said Observer Steve Piotrow. "Each eighty-pound block landed on the roof with a reverberating thud."

The savage summer gust of 1996 smashed a sixty-three-year-old record wind for July (the old record of 110 miles per hour was set in 1933). No higher wind speed has ever been recorded on the Rockpile during the months of June, July, or August.

What Is the Difference between Miles per Hour and Knots?

When reporting wind data to the National Weather Service, the Mount Washington Observatory records speeds in knots rather than miles per hour. A knot is a unit of speed: one nautical mile per hour, which is equal to 1.15 miles per hour. (A nautical mile is the length of one minute of longitude at Earth's equator.)

Knots are typically used to measure the speed of ships or aircraft. In the days of wooden sailing ships, sailors estimated their speed across the water using knotted ropes. They tied a rope to a large "float" or chunk of wood, dumped the float overboard from the moving ship, and then counted the knots as the rope slipped through their hands. Today, of course, our measurements are a bit more precise.

Knots are a familiar unit on television newscasts up and down the coast during marine weather forecasts.

Sawdust from the Log

"Century Club, baby! Steve conquers a 125-mph gust and trudges around the observation deck. Mike was really close until he got winded. Meanwhile, our crazy cat Nin jumps up on the weather desk about 6,000 times."

Fog

On Mount Washington, the sun is a rare sight in any season. Sometimes a week passes, and all we see is a pale white orb, drowned in deep fog. Three hundred days per year, the summit pokes through the clouds, wrapping the rocks in a sheet of mist. Although, on a clear day, it's possible to see a hundred miles or more to the Adirondacks or to the rolling blue waves of the Atlantic, on a foggy day it's hard enough to see your own shoelaces.

Fog is a cloud on the ground. Each particle of fog is a tiny droplet of water less than 0.0006 inch in diameter. (To picture how small this really is, take a ruler, a pair of scissors, and a piece of string. Measure a one-inch length of string and try to cut it into ten equal-sized pieces. That's hard enough. But now, you must cut each individual piece a thousand times more—an impossible task.) By comparison, a typical raindrop is 0.08 inch in diameter, more than a hundred times larger. To compare the size of a raindrop to a "fogdrop," think of a basketball next to a pea.

Fog floats in the air; it is not heavy enough to fall like drizzle or rain. Fog (and clouds) form when the air cools to its dew point and becomes "saturated" with water. The dew point is the temperature at which condensation outpaces evaporation, allowing fog (or dew) to form.

Warm air is sometimes said to have more of a "holding capacity" for water vapor, but the phrase "holding capacity" is figurative. A certain meteorology professor at Penn State will scold me if I fail to explain that nitrogen and oxygen molecules in the air don't "hold" the water vapor molecules in the air. The water is constantly changing phase—evaporating and condensing—independently of the oxygen and nitrogen.

The more accurate, technical explanation involves the relative rates of condensation versus evaporation in fluctuating temperatures. If you warm up the air, it will "hold" more water vapor only in the sense that there will be more molecules present with enough energy to remain in the gaseous state as water vapor. Cool the air and you get more water condensing to a liquid state. But the usual response of a layperson upon hearing the technical explanation is "Huh?" That's why most weather books, including this one, poetically say that warm air "holds" more water vapor than cold air does. In other words, it takes fewer water vapor molecules to "saturate" the air at, say, 40°F than it does at 80°F. When the air is "saturated" (I'll pause a moment while the meteorology professors roll their eyes) at 100 percent relative humidity, the water vapor in the air condenses and fog appears.

Fog is really just an ocean of tiny water droplets afloat in the air. If we could somehow shove all this fog into a compression tank and squeeze it, we could wring out enough water or snow to fill a lake. Clouds appear light and airy, afloat in the sky like clumps of white wool. But clouds do have weight. If you could wring dry a typical cumulus cloud, you would end up with thousands of pounds of water. Even without clouds or fog, the air is still full of moisture, especially on a hot, humid day. All across the planet, some 200 billion tons of water vapor evaporate off the ocean every hour. Later, some of that moisture condenses in the form of clouds and falls as rain or snow.

Not all fog is alike. Ground fog, radiation fog, and sea fog are just a few of many types of fog. Sometimes fog is wet, so wet you think you could practically swim the backstroke through the air. Other times it is relatively dry and thin. In particularly cold regions, where the mercury huddles in the bottom of the thermometer, ice fog can appear. Ice fog is composed of tiny ice particles, unlike normal fog, which is tiny water droplets suspended in the air. Ice fog usually forms at temperatures of -20°F or colder and does not produce rime, which is soft, crumbly ice.

Rime, in a poetic sense, is "frozen cloud." You'll also hear it referred to as "freezing fog," which gets coded on the Observatory's hourly METAR reports as FZFG. Pun-prone summit crew members may joke about there being "no rime or reason" to the weather, but in truth there's plenty of rime, most of the time.

One brisk, foggy day, I hiked to the summit, and as soon as I reached the Alpine Garden, the clouds lifted. Bright sunshine cut through the fog; shadows sprang from the boulders. I squinted into the glare and saw rime everywhere. Anything that previously had been in the fog— boulders, signposts, and even my jacket—now was covered with a white, feathery ice.

Rime is the solid residue of supercooled fog. It grows into the wind. Spears of rime appear whenever the air is thick with fog, the wind is blowing, and the temperature dips below 32°F. Most of the white you see when you look up at the summit cone in early winter comes from rime rather than snow.

I remember another cold, wet day in June, when billows of fog fluttered in the breeze. Visibility on the summit dropped to less than fifty feet, erasing the distant hills. Hikers who strayed too far from the trail quickly vanished in the mist. Around noontime, a single weary backpacker stumbled through the door of the Sherman Adams summit building and shook raindrops off the sleeve of his parka. A puddle oozed across the floor. The man looked for a ranger, walked over to introduce himself, and then asked, out-of breath, "Is this the bottom?"

Sawdust from the Log
June

"Where's the butter knife, we need to cut through this fog. Visibility is down to 25 feet. A couple of lightning crashes sound like they directly hit the tower."

Lightning and Thunder

Lightning is no stranger here; the radio towers perched on the peaks are frequent targets. Thunderstorms sometimes ignite them like giant metal candles. Tall, billowing, towering cumulus clouds, which can grow very rapidly into thunderstorms, are signs of an unstable atmosphere. "Stable" air is flat, horizontal, while "unstable" air has a lot of vertical motion. ("Towering cumulus" is a technical term, not a gratuitous adjective. Check the hourly coded weather reports from Mount Washington in the summer and you'll often see the code TCU ALQDS, which means "towering cumulus, all quadrants.")

Folklore refers to towering cumulus clouds: "When the sky is filled with rocks and towers, the earth's refreshed with frequent showers." There's a lot of churning inside these clouds, jostling small cloud droplets together to form larger raindrops. As the air rises, eventually it cools near the top of the cloud and becomes denser—and denser air starts to

**TOWERING CUMULUS CLOUDS CAN GROW
RAPIDLY INTO THUNDERSTORMS.**

sink. Falling snow or raindrops within the clouds can also create a suction, "dragging" air behind them. Often at the edge of a thunderstorm, or when the cloud is in its dying stages, you'll experience downdrafts or microbursts. The latter is a sudden blast of cold air, directed downward. There are often downdrafts at the front and rear flanks of a towering cumulus or cumulonimbus, with updrafts in the center.

Down in the kitchen on a summer night, the Observatory crew heard the wind suddenly surge and growl. A hiss of air whistled through the tower door.

"Is the three-cup down?" asked Ken Rancourt. Outside, the winds were gusting to fifty miles per hour, strong enough to break twigs off trees. Our fragile three-cup anemometer (used to measure low wind speeds) was unlikely to survive in such strong winds.

No one remembered taking down the three-cup. "It's probably blown away to North Conway by now," said Ken.

Since I was on duty, the chore of rescuing the anemometer fell to me. Lucky me. I put down my fork next to a half-finished slice of eggplant parmesan and ran upstairs.

When I pushed open the door at the top of the tower, a spittle of rain struck my face. My flashlight cut a long yellow beam in the fog; I wielded it like a sword, dissecting the night. My foot splashed in a puddle on the parapet.

Off to one side, an unexpected light blinked once and was gone. But when I turned to look, the sky was black and empty. "Was it lightning?" I wondered. No storm was expected that night, and I heard no distant thunder, just the roar of the wind. Surely it was just a stray reflection, the glow of my flashlight on the watery walls.

Up top, the three-cup spun in a frenzy, too fast to see. It hummed like an angry bee and barely registered as a blur in my flashlight beam. I reached up to pull it down . . .

The sky exploded. Just inches over my head, the sky burst into flame, or so it seemed. Ribbons of electricity sizzled along the eastern skyline, igniting the Maine border for a hundred miles. Fear jolted me and raised the hairs on my arms. Mount Washington was poking into the very heart of a thunderstorm. What a predicament: to be standing on the highest point in New England, clutching a metal anemometer, while forks of lightning speared the sky!

Rain trickled down my face; I wiped the water away with a sleeve. I groped for the metal nut that holds the three-cup in place, but my hands slipped on the slick, wet surface. No matter how much I twisted and turned it, it would not come loose. The sky shook with thunder, as if to say, "This is your last warning!"

Cloud-to-cloud lightning blazed directly above me. Sheets of white electricity snapped in the fog. At last I pulled the nut free, snatched the suddenly quiet three-cup from its post, and ran. I leapt off the last rung of the ladder, slipped on a puddle at the edge of the parapet, and ended up squat on the ground. Then, at last, I was safe inside.

I slammed the door shut and bolted it, then slumped to the floor in the Cold Room. My legs felt as if the bones had been drained of marrow, seeming too weak to support my weight. For a second, I just leaned against the wall of two-foot-thick reinforced concrete, regaining my equilibrium while the unexpected storm raged outside.

"Thundersnow!" gets written in the logbook during rare winter thunderstorms. We once accidentally fried a computer—and nearly fried one of the observers as well—when a February thunderstorm sneaked up on the summit. Anna Porter Johnston was de-icing the instruments at the top of the observation tower when the storm struck. She saw a spark out of the corner of her eye and worried that she had accidentally shorted something out. A second nearby flash was unmistakably lightning—and there she was on the highest point for a thousand miles, holding a metal bar. She got back inside safely, and quickly.

Does a lightning bolt shoot up or down? To the naked eye, lightning appears to droop from the sky like a fiery vine; each string of electricity dangles off the bottom edge of a cloud. The ancient Greeks imagined Zeus sitting on his throne high on Mount Olympus, hurling lightning bolts at his enemies.

Actually, what we *see* as lightning is a phenomenon called the return stroke, a sudden surge of positive energy traveling up from the ground. But the initial, deadly bolt of lightning is invisible, a stealthy strip of negative energy dropping from the clouds. This "invisible lightning" precedes the brightly lit return stroke by just a fraction of a second.

Can we tell how far away a lightning storm is? Lightning and thunder occur at the same time, of course, but because light travels so much faster than sound, we see lightning a few seconds before we hear thunder. Light reaches our eyes at the astonishing speed of 186,000 miles per second. Sound waves are more sluggish; they must plod through the atmosphere at a "mere" 980 feet per second. (This is an average speed; variations in temperature and air density affect the speed of sound.)

Sound waves travel one mile in about five seconds. To determine how far away the lightning flash occurred, start to count as soon as you see it strike. If you hear thunder two or three seconds later, the lightning strike was only half a mile away. Ten seconds later, two miles away.

Thunder "grumbles" because the sound reaches us at slightly different times from varying points up and down the lightning bolt. Thunder that originates close to the ground will reach us sooner than thunder high in the sky.

What causes thunder? Lighting is hot: nearly 50,000°F, hotter than the photosphere, the surface of the sun. A lightning bolt heats the fluid air around it and causes it to expand. Heated, agitated air scatters in all directions but quickly encounters cooler air and cools back to normal temperatures. As it cools, the air contracts and "claps" back together. We hear this clap as thunder.

On the Brighter Days

Fortunately, there is more in Mother Nature's kitchen than pea-soup fog and killer winds. She occasionally cooks up bright days and clear nights, even on Mount Washington. One entry in the logbook shows the weather's good side:

"April 10, 1997. Celestial madness!!! Today was one of those days that reminds us why we're here. We set a record cold temperature of -8°F in the morning, had a peak wind gust of 108 mph a few hours later, enjoyed 100-mile visibility in the afternoon, and were treated to a once-in-a-lifetime celestial display consisting of the Hale-Bopp comet, a dazzling curtain of aurora borealis, a crescent moon, and shooting stars after sunset."

We spend a lot of time looking at the sky, especially when there is a good likelihood of meteor showers. Meteors, or "shooting stars," are caused by chunks of asteroids that enter Earth's atmosphere. Friction with air molecules creates tremendous heat, which incinerates them in the upper atmosphere. Most people hear the

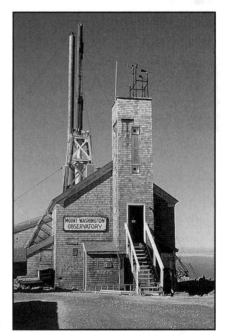

THE OLD OBSERVATORY BUILDING ON A RARE SUNNY DAY.

word *meteor* and think of shooting stars. Seen from the ground, a meteor does look like a star streaking across the sky. Occasionally, a bit of rock survives its fiery plunge and strikes Earth's surface as a meteorite.

The science of meteorology is all about weather, not about those incandescent pebbles from outer space that entertain us on clear nights. So why is the study of rain and clouds called *meteor*ology? The term comes from an ancient book by Aristotle called *Meteorologica*. *Meteor* is Greek for "in the sky," and *ology* means "study of." Thus, meteorology is "the study of things in the sky." A clever crew member at the Observatory might try to use that loophole to get away with idly watching the ravens swoop and soar in the sky outside the weather room window instead of doing paperwork. Ravens are things in the sky, aren't they? "I'm doing meteorology right now! Honest." (Summit cats Marty and Nin both like to perch on the radiator by the window and "study" this type of meteorology intently.)

In many ways, Aristotle was the world's first weatherman. But like every other weather observer in the world, he was known to blow a forecast or two. He also mixed up his facts. Aristotle believed that comets were atmospheric phenomena, just like clouds. Little did he know that they are actually giant, distant ice balls in highly elliptical orbits around the sun.

In the science of meteorology, a hydrometeor is made of water in the air, such as rain, snow, or hail. A lithometeor is made of solid dry particles, such as dust, smoke, or (in certain instances) volcanic ash. Haze is also a lithometeor; it is formed by tiny particles such as pollen or pollution and casts a dark-bluish veil over the landscape.

In a sense, a "shooting star" is also a lithometeor. Although we weather watchers on Mount Washington are more concerned with fog and haze than with asteroid debris or flying snowballs in outer space, we still take the time to admire shooting stars on cold, clear nights.

Once while I was working the night shift, the phone rang—a rattle of bells in the night. The caller told me to look up at the sky. I wrote down in the logbook what I saw: "Shooting stars galore. Someone calls up and asks if we saw a meteor with a green tail and a red nose. We were in the fog at the time, so we didn't see much of anything. Probably it was Rudolph making a test run."

Sawdust from the Log
Late 1985

"Halley's (rhymes with valley) Comet (rhymes with . . . you know) was spotted in 11-by-80 binoculars on a tripod. Only a faint coma is visible, as it is pointed straight at us at this time. It was very dim and at the limit of vision. Art said, 'Is that all there is?' Al could not see it at all, and Ken didn't even try to look."

Our rare clear-sky days give the Observatory summit dwellers treasured opportunities to witness a variety of spectacular and colorful phenomena. Sunsets paint the clouds with brilliant reds and oranges. Clouds churn in the sky like flames, ignited by the sun. More clouds stampede across the valleys below, and the higher summits poke through to the sky like islands in the sea. I stare at the first glimmers of twilight from the top of the tower, my hair rustled by a light wind. The orange circle of the sun hangs over the hills, dripping fiery drops into a chasm below the horizon. Earth seems to roll faster as night nears; the sun and mountains below me stampede deep into the shadows. Quickly, the sun is squashed into an oval against the distant hills of New York.

In the valleys, constellations of brightly lit lakes sparkle and wink off one by one. Soon the sun is just a puddle of light, a distant lake of fire tucked between two mountains. Night is closing in. Finally, the sun sits in a groove of mountains, a dull red coal emitting its last flicker. Just before it dies, as the last lip of fire licks the horizon, we see a colorful glow—the so-called green flash.

"There it goes—poof—just like that," says a ranger, leaning against the tower's parapet. "With any luck, it'll be back again tomorrow," he adds.

What is the green flash? At dusk on a clear night, the last sliver of sun will glow a pale green as it dips below the horizon. The sun's light is being refracted or bent in the atmosphere, split into many colors, like light through a prism. For a brief instant, we see the green portion of the spectrum.

The flash is best seen through binoculars (but be careful not to look until the very last sliver of the sun sinks below the horizon; it is dangerous to look directly at the sun). The effect lasts for only a pale second and can be seen only in a clear sky, either from a mountaintop or looking across a flat surface like the ocean. Of course, since Mount Washington has its nose in the clouds 300 days a year, seeing the green flash at sunset is a rare treat for the Observatory crew.

Ice

The average daily temperature at the summit of Mount Washington in September is 40.4°F, but in October, the air chills to an average of 30.2°F, with overnight lows well below freezing. And that means it is time for rime, snow flurries, and freezing rain as we leave summer behind and move into colder seasons. Officially, the meteorological winter begins on December 1 (the "calendar" winter starts on the winter solstice, on or around December 21.) But sometimes, it feels as though winter lasts from September to all the way through May. Eleven inches of snow typically falls in May.

What is freezing rain? Rain that falls as a liquid but freezes on impact is called freezing rain, designated by the abbreviation FZRA on the hourly weather reports, or "obs," compiled by the Observatory staff. It might seem strange that liquid water can fall when the air temperature is below 32°F, but that's exactly what happens. The liquid cools to below freezing, and as soon as it hits the Observatory tower or the rocks, it solidifies into a treacherously slippery sheet of ice.

Glaze ice and rime ice. Glaze ice is like glass—hard, clear, and slippery. It is formed by the splatter of freezing rain on freezing drizzle. Rime, on the other hand, is feathery thin, soft, and easily crumbled.

FEATHERY RIME ICE TRANSFORMS THE
SUMMIT INTO AN ARCTIC LANDSCAPE.

Rime forms from fog. With the summit of Mount Washington so often in the fog, supercooled cloud droplets freeze on contact with anything solid: rocks, walls, people, cats—and scientific instruments, too. Rime is basically "frozen cloud." It consists of tiny bubbles of cold air wrapped in ice. Spears of rime grow into the wind, and it's not uncommon to have a six-foot-long shaft of rime reaching over the edge of the tower, like the giant white arm of the Yeti, the Abominable Snowman.

One of the Observatory's many research projects is to measure the accumulation of ice on a device called a multicylinder. From this data, we can study the size and formation of cloud droplets.

Both rime and glaze ice encase the instruments and must constantly be hammered off to ensure accurate readings. Gauges and anemometers are not accurate if encased in rime, so the crew at the Observatory works up a sweat hammering ice off the tower. It was rime ice on the anemometer that compelled Sal Pagliuca to stand atop the tower in a 200-mph wind in 1934.

It comes as no surprise that the summits of the White Mountains see plenty of snow. A typical December dumps 55 inches of snow on the summit, though in 1968, 103.7 inches fell in that month alone. In fact, the winter of 1968–69 was the snowiest one on record, with 566.4 inches all told.

Let's compare a "real" winter to a winter in Caribou, Maine, a town where people are said to spend more time driving snowmobiles than cars. For good measure, we'll throw in statistics from Boston as well. Here is the way the numbers add up for February 1969, one of the snowiest months in New England history:

February 1969	Mount Washington	Caribou	Boston
Average temperature	8.2°F	17.7°F	29.7°F
High temperature	34°	43°	40°
Low temperature	-25°	-20°	12°
Snow accumulation	172.8″	29.7″	41.3″
Greatest 24-hour snowfall	49.3″	12.8″	13.7″

Here is how Mount Washington weather stacks up against Boston and Caribou all year round:

Year-round	Mount Washington	Caribou	Boston
Average annual temperature	27.2°F	38.8°F	51.5°F
All-time high temperature	72°	96°	104°
All-time low temperature	-47°	-41°	-12°
Average wind speed	35.3 mph	11.2 mph	12.5 mph
Highest wind speed	231 mph	76 mph	76 mph
Average yearly snowfall	314.8″	110″	40″
Greatest annual snowfall	566.4″	181″	108″

What makes it cold, anyway? Cold, or heat, is a matter of kinetic energy, a measure of how fast atoms and molecules move. Heat things up, and molecules move faster. In the cold blackness of outer space, the temperature comes close to absolute zero, at which point even the innards of atoms shrivel up and freeze. Absolute zero is -459.67°F. At such a temperature, nothing moves at all.

A good example of energy in motion is an Observatory crew member shooting down the mountain on a sled. What a way to commute home from work! The sledder has kinetic energy when he is in motion, but potential energy when perched at the top of the mountain, waiting for a shove on the back to get moving. ("A sledder has the potential to break his neck, hence potential energy," jokes an observer.)

Sawdust from the Log
December 4, 1988

"Dana goes out on the roof in sneakers to measure the rods. The 80-mph winds blow him to the rotunda with his sneakers acting like skis on the icy ground. He throws himself flat and must crawl back for lack of traction. Quite an adventure!"

Measuring Temperature

The familiar Fahrenheit scale, widely used in the United States, was invented by Gabriel Fahrenheit in 1714. Most of the rest of the world, including our neighbors in Canada, use the Celsius scale, which was invented by Anders Celsius in 1742.

In the Celsius scale, water boils at 100 and freezes at 0 (at standard pressure at sea level). In Fahrenheit, the temperatures are 212 and 32, respectively. If the temperature drops far enough, the two scales meet at -40°.

It Could Be Worse

Weather in the North Country is always unpredictable. During the summer months—July and August—kaleidoscopes of clouds reel overhead, depositing rain, hail, fog, and drops of sunlight in equal measure. The rest of the time, in spring, fall, and winter, frost, sleet, and snow are the norm.

"You have winter nine months of the year!" groans a friend of mine from Seattle, peeking out from under her mandatory umbrella. And I confess, it's true; in some places, like the bowl of Tuckerman Ravine, the snow season can last until late July. Dedicated skiers can hunt for lingering patches of snow on the mountain and sometimes get in a few turns even in summer. But it wasn't always so. One year, according to weather folklore, summer never came at all.

In 1816, drought and unseasonable cold tormented farmers throughout the Northeast. Winter stubbornly refused to yield to spring. At the same time, to everyone's dismay, a mysterious black spot appeared on the sun. Swarms of smaller spots could also be seen, plainly visible to the naked eye. Clearly something was wrong.

Were celestial apparitions to blame for the never-ending season of snow and cold? Many thought so and panicked. Down in Massachusetts, one amateur astronomer claimed to have seen a sunspot explode before his eyes. "The appearance was that of a piece of ice which, when dashed on a frozen pond, breaks to pieces, and slides in every direction."

Such apocalyptic visions did little to soothe people's fears. At dawn and dusk, the life-giving sun glowed a pale, sickly orange, blotted with spots, as if it had caught a pox. To make matters worse, frost and snow squalls struck northern New England in May, June, and July, while killing frosts damaged or destroyed crops from the Berkshires and Connecticut to Maine. People wondered, was the sun ill? Were blemishes on the sun's surface preventing light and heat from reaching Earth?

Actually, the grim weather of 1816 is now mostly blamed on large quantities of dust and aerosols in the upper atmosphere, spewed from a volcanic eruption in the Dutch East Indies (today's Indonesia) the year before.

Whatever effects the sunspot activity also may have had on the climate is still uncertain, but the dust from the 1815 eruption of Mount

Tambora certainly dimmed the sun, making its dark spots easier to see with the naked eye. Many people who had never noticed sunspots before suddenly became aware of them, while astronomers pondered possible relationships between sunspot activity and peculiarities in the weather.

We know today that sunspots are merely large, cool regions of the sun's photosphere, not portents of impending doom. But in 1816, laymen knew nothing about solar mechanics, and astronomers knew little more.

With typical Yankee humor, a newspaper column poked fun at the raging debate: "The *phenomenon* which has excited so much astonishment . . . is a large *pumkpin.*" This theory about sunspots and cold weather was advanced by a "Mr. Philander Sarcasm" in newspapers around the country. As Mr. Sarcasm explained, the giant solar pumpkin dangled from a vine "of sufficient length to reach below the circumambient atmosphere of the sun" and thus be visible from Earth. He added, "It will be visible every revolution of the Sun, until it is gathered."

Apparently someone harvested the celestial pumpkin in late autumn. By 1817, sunspot sightings decreased significantly, volcanic dust and aerosols in the stratosphere started to dissipate, and the weather returned to what passes for normal in New England.

Part II

Seasons

ICE MELTS IN THE SPRING SUN ABOVE A SEA OF CLOUDS.

Chapter 3

Spring

WINTER-LIKE WEATHER IS ALWAYS A threat on the summit of Mount Washington, and sometimes the ice is reluctant to slacken its grip come spring. The average overnight low temperature on the mountain is only 5.9°F in March, with frequent dips below zero. Snow continues to fall with all the intensity of winter. But the thaw is on nonetheless; cold rain finally starts to wash away the rime in April and May.

Deep snowdrifts make it necessary for the Observatory crew to use the Bombardier to travel up and down the mountain. On an unusually warm day in 1992, one meteorologist noted in the Observatory logbook: "Came up today in deep slush and water. At times the Sno-Cat would plow through a four-foot-deep river of slush, with water gushing over the treads."

Later, when a cold front passed through, he wrote: "Snow, snow, snow . . . oh let it blow." As March edged into April that year, winter conditions still prevailed: "The blizzard wasn't as bad as I expected," reads another entry in the logbook, "but we did have a peak gust of 145 mph. It took quite a bit of work to go outside. The wind knifed right through my jacket, pants, and overmitts. I had snow buildup on the *inside* of my goggles."

Finally, in April and May, warm breezes melt away half a year's worth of snow and ice. Talk about change! Creeks full of cold water gurgle down the rocky mountain slopes and wash the boulders clean. Dark spikes of rock poke up through a roof of melting snow. All across New England, the ground thaws and rivers ripple and surge with the runoff of melting snow. In the valleys, maple branches sprout buds and the first flowers bloom. The air carries a gentle breeze, a warm sigh of relief after the cold gusts of winter.

On Mount Washington, the average temperature in May is still only 35.6°F, but that's a steep rise from the chilly 22.9°F of April and the 13.6°F typical of March. For the first time in many months, above-freezing temperatures become common—especially in mid-afternoon, when the sun's hot rays pour down on the rocks.

After a long, icy winter huddled inside the Observatory's concrete walls, what a relief it is to "dress down" into a mere wool sweater, rather than the usual combination of heavy parka, facemask, wind pants, and goggles. But not everyone on the mountaintop is pleased. I once saw a message scribbled in the pages of the logbook: "Winter disappears over-night. Whoever took away the snow better bring it back real soon."

Perhaps those grumblers miss the end of sledding season. A delight-ful perk of life on the summit is the chance to sled down the mountain. Where else in the world, aside from an Olympic luge competition, can you enjoy an uninterrupted eight-mile sled run? (Unfortunately, the sleds don't work too well on the trip back up.) You've heard the old say-ing, "April showers bring May flowers." On Mount Washington, April flurries bring May worries—and also provide a last chance to play in the snow before the warm breath of summer melts it all away.

It is late May, and a thin layer of hail and ice cakes the ground. With winds gusting to 75 miles per hour, a young crew member bundles into a heavy parka and steps outside. The wind whooshes the door out of his hand and slams it shut; a metallic echo shudders through the Sherman Adams building. Instantly, fingers of wind snatch his shoulders and fling him away from the door. To stop, he stoops and curls into a ball, drag-ging his gloves against the ground. Rime ice clings to his hat, and his bright blue jacket turns white with snow, sparkling in the moonlight. Undeterred, the meteorologist tucks a red plastic sled under his arm and

MARK ROSS-PARENT

SLEDDING IS A FAVORITE PASTIME OF THE SUMMIT CREW.

hauls it to the edge of the observation deck. Finally, he kneels in the sled, holding out his arms like a ship's spars. Wind puffs up his jacket like a ship's sails and nudges him quickly across the deck. His sleigh ride across the ice ends in a pile of snow a few seconds later.

After a long, brutal winter, the temperature suddenly shoots above freezing. In the minds of the summit crew, a heat wave of 40°F feels just like the Bahamas.

During the warmest days of the spring thaw, meteorologists on Mount Washington start to melt away like snowmen. Spring thaw changes the tasks at hand. Icing research projects are put in mothballs until the snow flies again. In the old days (before the 2003 fire), our neighbors in the TV-8 transmitter building would emerge from their icy cocoon and stroll across the peak. Far down the slope, bulldozers and plows help the Auto Road crew carve a path through lingering layers of snow and ice.

Opening day for the visitor center is not far away. In May, doors that have been sealed shut all winter are cracked open in preparation for the summer tourist season. Visitors from southern New England start to climb to the peak, taunting the isolated summit-dwellers with visions of dandelions in the grass. But no dandelions grow in the rocky world above treeline, where sedges and grasses stay brown until mid-June. Instead, each June, arctic flowers left over from the last ice age suddenly wink open on the peaks. Stranded above timberline, clumps of half-open diapensia blossoms yawn at the sky. Their white petals shine in the sun.

The reappearance of the sun after endless months of being buried in fog is just one of the many changes for weather observers on top of Mount Washington. Since a typical winter dumps more than 314 inches of snow on the mountain, it comes as a bit of a shock when warm, wet water droplets start to plummet from the sky. "What do you call it? Rain?" asks a puzzled mountain meteorologist, shaking his head.

The idea of "unfrozen precipitation" takes a bit of getting used to, but pretty soon we have rainwater up to our ears. When the first downpour or thunderstorm clobbers the mountain, the Observatory watchtower fills with water like a giant canteen. Melting snow dribbles through cracks in the cement, and rainwater gushes down the hatch from the parapet. Inside, the cold cement walls drip and run. "We have heavy rain showers inside the tower," someone shouts. "Time to start building an ark!"

As I climb up the ladder to the Cold Room, fat drops trickle off the rungs of the ladder and fall with a plunk in a puddle at the bottom. Other drops splat against my face. A cold shower of rainwater mats my hair. And yet, here I am, safely inside a building, with a thick concrete roof overhead.

During a spring thunderstorm, the Observatory tower feels like the innards of submarine, its walls squeezed by the immense pressure of the ocean. Water percolates off the walls, and a constant dripping noise plunks in the background. "Man the lifeboats, start bailing," reads an entry in the logbook. Sometimes it's hard to believe we are more than a mile above sea level. When the highest point in New England starts to flood, you know that spring and summer are here at last.

Sawdust from the Log
June 19, 1995

"Oh the heat was practically unbearable today! We broke a record by hitting 67°F. Down at Lakes of the Clouds, a hiker fell on the rocks and badly cut herself. Observatory and State Park folks carried her in a litter to the summit, where she was evacuated to a hospital via the Auto Road."

SEAN DOUCETTE / MOUNT WASHINGTON OBSERVATORY

IN THE WHITE MOUNTAINS, APRIL SNOW
SHOWERS BRING MAY FLOWERS.

SOME VISITORS TRAVEL TO THE SUMMIT BY CAR OR COG.
OTHERS COME ON FOOT . . . OR HOOF.

Chapter 4

Summer

IN SUMMER, ICICLES FINALLY MELT and drip into the rocks. When the fog clears, boulders studded with glassy minerals start to glitter in the sun.

Summertime is a mix of bustling activity and quiet contemplation on Mount Washington. A thoughtful weather observer wrote in the logbook on July 7, 1994, "Today was quiet on the summit, as fog and rain showers kept most of the visitors at home."

Transportation up the Mount Washington Auto Road is easier in the summer, but only slightly less precarious. In places, the narrow, twisting road to the summit skirts uncomfortably close to the edge. Volunteer Kristy Medeiros laughs as she describes her trip up the road in a van: "I forgot how scary it can be when you get above the treeline. Barry can show you the bruise on his leg from me grabbing on."

It was foggy when she arrived on the summit on June 12, 2008, but skies cleared the next day. "We went outside every chance we had," remembers Kristy. "The observers tell you to take advantage of the good weather. You could be fogged in for days; you never know." The crew's advice was to walk down the Auto Road. "Something easy," says Kristy. But soon the wind picked up, and it turned out to be not so easy after all. "Every time I took a step, the wind would blow one foot into the other. Very weird."

Snowfields were visible from Homestretch, and as soon as she got back to the Observatory, two interns announced that they were going skiing. "Come watch, they told me. Are you kidding?" She found a nice rock to sit on and watched them ski and snowboard. "I was getting mad that I didn't bring my skis," says Kristy. But who expects to get a chance to go skiing in mid-June?

One of the skiers woke up Kristy and her husband Barry the next morning at 4 a.m. to see a spectacular sight. "Because of the way the sun rises with some clouds, Mount Washington casts a shadow in the sky." The triangular shadow of the mountain spears across the miles toward Vermont, with a halo, or "glory," near the top.

The phenomenon is named after the Brocken, a peak in Germany's Harz Mountains. Many climbers reported seeing ghostly images in the fog. Hikers on a high ridge, as they gazed down at the clouds below, saw their shadows projected on the mist as the low-lying sun slowly rose behind them.

An awe-inspiring sight, but you have to get up early to see brocken spectres and

A BROCKEN SPECTRE AND GLORY AT SUNRISE.

glories on Mount Washington. "Back to bed we go," thought Kristy. Only she had to get right back up a moment later when Marty the cat started scratching at the bunkroom door. "Let him in so he can cuddle," said a half-asleep Kristy.

Sawdust from the Blog
Summer 2006

"Again this morning in the undercast shone another spectacular brocken spectre and glory, a real treat to see for those early hikers."

The appeal of the mountain on hot, muggy July days can be summed up in three words: natural air conditioning. While the valleys boil away in 90-degree heat, we might enjoy a relatively cool 55°F. Never has the mercury risen above 72°F on this mountain. Usually, even in the summer, it stays in the 40s and 50s.

In summer, fields of tundra grass still ripple and writhe in the wind. Icy fingers of wind still poke and prod the boulders. On average, only an inch of snow falls in June, with just a few flurries in July and August. Unfortunately, many hikers come unprepared for the possibility of sub-arctic conditions. They forget that even in summer, Old Man Winter sometimes sneaks up on the summit and wraps his icy arms around unsuspecting travelers. Accidents and deaths occur in the mountains in all seasons, so the Observatory staff and State Park crew are always on call, cooperating in search-and-rescue operations.

Sawdust from the Blog
August 2008

"My bunkroom is in the corner of the building at the bottom of the tower, so when I went to bed last night I could hear the wind howling outside. This morning I was awoken around 4:30 by a steady thwacking noise reverberating down from the tower. I realized that the thwacking could only mean one thing: icing."

Three hikers were unprepared when the weather turned savage in June 2008. They reached the summit late, long after they should have made the safe choice and turned back. There's no shelter for hikers on the summit, not after dark. The doors were locked, the fog was so thick it was almost solid, and no one could hear them knocking. "They found an unlocked vehicle and huddled inside for warmth," recalls Kristy Medeiors, that week's summit volunteer. She warmed them up with hot coffee. "They sat at the table this morning like three little wet puppy dogs who did wrong."

Summer days bring swarms of visitors, as sightseers and hikers congregate on the top of Mount Washington. But is there any pity for our poor, windblown summit staff? Each morning on shift-change day, after all the rangers, meteorologists, and other employees battle their way through savage gusts to reach the Sherman Adams summit building, they immediately encounter a barrage of questions, comments, and complaints.

"Do you ever get any moose up here?" a tall man from downstate once asked. He leaned on the countertop with his elbows and pointed to the piles of mica schist boulders with a thrust of his chin. "Yes, we do get moose above treeline," the ranger answered. "Not often, though." The man paused; his chin drooped. Finally he inquired, "How do you get them up here?"

Workers on the summit—park rangers, gift shop employees, and meteorologists from the Mount Washington Observatory—have compiled a list of odd, amusing, or alarming questions put to them by tourists. The list circulates amid gales of puzzled laughter during the off-hours.

"Can I park my car on the roof?"

"Are these mountains above sea level?"

"This is my first time up Mount Washington. What am I supposed to do?"

A young, ponytailed visitor once stepped up to the ranger's desk with an important question: "Do you have a microwave oven?" When the ranger replied in the affirmative, she asked, "Can I use it to dry my boyfriend's pants?"

The most common question is, "Where are all the president's faces?" Visitors who have driven to New Hampshire's mountains from afar are never pleased to learn that Mount Rushmore is sixteen hundred miles away. Mount Washington may be named for our first president, but its stones are not etched in his image. Perhaps a subconscious mixing up of the Presidential Range (of which Mount Washington is a part) and the Old Man of the Mountain (the famous, face-like rocky outcropping that was in New Hampshire's Franconia Notch) is what causes the occasional visitor to search for Mount Rushmore in New Hampshire. I suspect we'll hear this question less often from now on. The Old Man of the Mountain eroded and fell in a heap of broken rock in 2003.

"Is this the tallest mountain in the state of Washington?" other visitors have asked.

"Do you work for the state of Connecticut?"

"Who runs this place, the state of Vermont?"

"Can we see New Hampshire from here?"

Since Mount Washington lies along the Appalachian Trail, it is often visited by through-hikers on their way from Georgia to Mount Katahdin in Maine. Such well-traveled hikers can be identified by sight and (especially) smell, and other "normal" sightseers are often curious about them: "After they hike up the two-thousand-mile-long Appalachian Trail, how do they get back down?"

"Are the trails lit for night hiking?"

"Do you have an elevator to the base?"

In the end, of course, Mount Washington will always be most famous for its winds and weather. "Is it always this windy up here?" hikers usually ask.

"You claim this place has the world's worst weather. I always thought Philadelphia did."

"Is there any danger of this mountain erupting while I'm on it?"

In ancient times, people climbed mountains to ask wise hermits for advice. But today, things are different. Instead of long-bearded gurus, young park rangers and weather observers inhabit our mountaintops. So visitors should feel free to ask any questions. But remember: Up on Mount Washington, at least, the answers really *are* blowing in the wind.

Sawdust from the Log
June 20, 1996

"Nin, the incredible hiking cat, conquers Mount Clay this morning (meower power). Humans Matt and Jake tag along."

TIME-LAPSE PHOTOGRAPHY CAPTURES STAR TRAILS
ABOVE THE OBSERVATORY TOWER.

Chapter 5

Autumn

Sawdust from the Blog
September 2002

"It's been a warm clear night ... perfect for stargazing. The moon has just risen and it is a spectacularly red sliver of a crescent. We'd better appreciate these mild nights while we can ... fall's coming!"

"IT'S COAT SEASON OUT THERE," complains a tall, bearded man bundled up like an Eskimo in a heavy parka but still shivering with cold. With a shaky arm, he yanks open the door to the Observatory and staggers back outside, nudged by a sudden gust of wind. His coat drips with cold rain, and a crust of glaze ice soon clings to his beard. Behind him, a hurricane-force breeze slams the door shut with a harsh metallic clang.

I step outside to see this remarkable weather for myself. After all, just yesterday there were sunbathers on the roof. Can the seasons change so quickly?

You bet they can. Snow and ice can turn to sunshine in a matter of minutes—and then turn back again. Walking across the observation deck, I watch as the last stars wink out, one by one, in the early morning sky. A fresh autumn wind blows raw against my face. I rub my hands for warmth, wishing I had worn gloves.

At six a.m., deep below the horizon, the sun leaks a trickle of dawn onto the sky. The first glint of golden light wafts on the breeze like the scent of honey from a faraway tree, but no warmth comes with it. I can feel goose bumps prickle my skin. A fresh sheet of ice cracks under my boots with every step, and the western half of the sky pulsates with fog. Low stratocumulus clouds wash up over the summit from time to time, splashing the rocks with mist. Despite a brief break in the clouds at sunrise, foul weather quickly returns.

Overhead, the sky hangs shaggy and low. Nimbostratus clouds gather in dark gray lumps, dangling precariously above the summit like stalactites about to break loose and fall. Such clouds always produce a steady rain or snow. Scattered clumps of fog often materialize just below the main base of the cloud as falling rain and moisture condense. These little islands of fog are called scud clouds.

All morning, snow pours from the sky in fat flakes, set aswirl by the wind. Though the calendar says it is only early September, winter appears to have arrived in full force. When I retreat to the weather room, I see a note in the logbook, jotted down in blue ink: "Start your Christmas shopping, the season's first snow fell today." I glance at the thermograph and read a temperature of only 28°F, just a few degrees south of the freezing mark. In the background, I hear a crew member usher in the winter season by whistling, "Let it snow, let it snow, let it snow."

Apparently winter is in a hurry this year. It forgot to wait for fall.

"When summer birds take their flight, summer goes with them," is an old gem of weather folklore. Our ancestors watched birds fly south each autumn, shortly before the first frosts. They learned that the migration of birds was an omen, indicating a time when summer's warm breezes give way to the cold embrace of winter.

On Mount Washington, the visitors disappear and migrate south long before the birds do. Snowstorms and cold drive away most tourists to more comfortable climates. The State Park seals its doors, and the Auto Road and Cog Railway close up shop for the season. Any hardy hikers and skiers who stay on the peaks must put away their summer hiking boots and dig out ice axes and crampons to give themselves a solid foothold on the ice.

In the Presidential Range, the switch from summer to winter gives little warning. Autumn is just a short, colorful prelude to winter. High atop the White Mountains, on cold September days, Old Man Winter scouts around the rocks and ravines, searching for good spots for avalanches. He reaches deep into his pockets and sprinkles a little snow on the peaks. If you are hiking in autumn, it pays to come prepared. After a virtually snow-free summer, Mount Washington can wake up under a blanket of snow or layer of ice at any time from late August to mid-September.

The season's first snow shower usually falls on Mount Washington by September 2—a day eagerly awaited by the crew at the Observatory. "Snow dances" under the full moon are not unheard of, though their actual effect on the weather is doubtful. Perhaps all that perspiration adds just enough moisture to the air to create snow. Whatever the reason, the Observatory crew welcomes snow; they have been deprived of the joy of sledding down the mountain for far too long.

Technically, early September is still summer—that is, everywhere but Mount Washington. Down in Boston, for example, the Red Sox are still wearing short-sleeve shirts as they pursue another World Series win. (A mere five years ago, that sentence would have read, "as they dash their fans' hopes in yet another doomed-from-the-start pennant race." How times have changed.) Meanwhile, on Mount Washington, winter weather hits a home run. Typically, two inches of snow falls in September, with fourteen more in October. But you can't rely on averages, not where the weather is concerned. In October 2005, a whopping 78.9 inches of snow fell on Mount Washington.

The return of severe weather opens the door (sometimes literally) to a variety of icing research opportunities. The Observatory is proud of its ongoing tradition of scientific study. An experiment nicknamed Cosmo counts incoming particles from the sun as they strike Earth. The goal of this forty-year-old project is to see whether solar activity truly does have an effect on global weather patterns.

The Observatory summit facility also houses experiments and research projects by the University of New Hampshire, the Federal Aeronautics Administration, the U.S. Army's Cold Regions Research and Engineering Laboratory (CRREL), and the Appalachian Mountain Club, among others.

Ever the observant scientists, the staff at the Mount Washington Observatory have concluded that fruits and vegetables can change the weather. "Bananas cause fog" is an accepted truth on the Rockpile. The evidence? As soon as banana bread comes out of the oven, clouds wash over the mountain, drowning the peak in fog. "And if someone eats the last banana on a foggy day, the mist immediately fades away and the sun comes back," explains crew member Lynne Host. At least, that is the theory. Further research is required. Please pass the banana bread.

Fall Foliage

"It's October—time for you to go down and paint the leaves," we jokingly tell interns, holding up a brush and a can of paint. (No one has fallen for that one yet.)

From the top of the tower, the Mount Washington Observatory crew is treated to a bird's-eye view of the most spectacular fall foliage in the world. At the foot of Mount Washington lies a canopy of maples, birches, and green pine trees, laced together by needles and twigs. The forest fits against the base of the mountain like a snug wooden shoe.

While weather observers with paintbrushes don't give the autumn leaves their color, observing the weather can tell you how bright the fall foliage might be. A rainy summer season nourishes the cells that provide pigment, or color, but a drought in summer is bad news. If you have ever forgotten to water a houseplant, you know it turns a sickly pale yellow. Trees in the wild behave much the same way. Pigments in the leaves are darker and richer when the trees have had more rainwater to drink.

Actually, the red and yellow pigments that appear in autumn leaves are there all the time, but in summer they are masked by green chlorophyll cells. When the chlorophyll fades during the short days and cold nights of fall, the leaves expose a prism of bright colors underneath the green. Chlorophyll is the basis of photosynthesis, the process by which leaves sip energy from sunlight. Each chlorophyll molecule grabs hold of a sunbeam and converts it to food.

In summer, chlorophyll is the dominant color: green. When the green color fades in autumn, a pigment called carotene paints some leaves orange. Xanthophyll creates yellow, while anthocyanins turn other leaves deep red and purple.

Sawdust from the Blog
September 21, 2001

"Snow cover and freezing fog transform the top of the Rockpile into a winter wonderland overnight. The local fox must be excited, too. I can see its prints running underneath the weather room window! This snow may make for tricky footing for hikers today as it is very wet and covering a thin layer of ice."

Chapter 6

Everybody's Favorite—Winter

"WELL, IF I'VE GOT TO be stuck someplace working on Christmas, I guess this is the place to be," announces an Observatory staffer one snowy December day. She stands at the edge of the Observatory tower and whirls a psychrometer in the crystal-blue air.

A thousand feet below the summit of Mount Washington, waves of misty cumulus clouds gush up the slopes and wash the boulders with a river of fog. High above the summit, the sky is still clear; a single wispy cirrus cloud dangles like a white string off the bottom of the sun. Off to the north, a small mountain stands wrapped in a white cocoon of snow. Ice crystals sparkle and glitter on the peak. The sky is a cold blue dome.

Daylight never lasts long in winter. Early in the evening, the setting sun tumbles and rolls across the western horizon. As it sinks out of sight, colorful spears of light shoot up into the sky, and the snowcapped mountains blush red. Slowly, night settles over New England.

The winter solstice—also known as the festival of lights—occurs on or around December 21, the longest night of the year. It is when winter officially begins. Once the solstice passes, the days start to lengthen and the nights shrink—but the bitter cold of winter still lingers.

"It's always tough to be away from family on the holiday," recalls former summit manager Sarah Long, but she and the rest of the Christmas crew made the best of it. "Nin got to see his one tree a year with the arrival of the Christmas tree, and we would carry the holiday dinner over to the TV building in the whipping winds and driving snow," says Sarah. "Almost lost the turkey and pie in those winds a couple of times!"

Cold and dark though it may be, the sky rarely fails to put on a show on Christmas Eve. Outside the Observatory, wind is an icy chisel, sculpting rime formations on the windows. Streams of gray fog cascade down the slopes of Mount Washington. Overhead, starlight and moonbeams wink on and off through holes in the clouds. Below the summit, an undercast of low stratocumulus surges against the hills. A few high peaks poke up through this white ocean like islands afloat in the sky.

No one escapes a hard day's work on the Rockpile just because the calendar says it's a holiday. Weather never stops; it is the power of our atmosphere in action. Meteorologists at the Mount Washington Observatory spend the winter holidays on a summit above the clouds, with plenty of time to contemplate the elements.

THE NORTHERN PRESIDENTIAL RANGE
(MT. JEFFERSON, MT. ADAMS, AND MT. MADISON)
EMERGES FROM THE UNDERCAST.

It's a long hike down to timberline (and an even longer hike back up) to get a Christmas tree to decorate, but the crew makes do. Staff meteorologist Ryan Knapp composed an ode during the Christmas shift on the summit in 2007:

'Twas the night before Christmas, and up on the summit
Temperatures were cold as they started to plummet.
Our stockings were hung below the TV with care,
In hopes that a man in red would soon be there.

The day shift was nestled all snug in their beds
While visions of cookie men danced in their heads.
And Nin in his box and me in my gear
Both dreamt that the morning soon would be here.

Here's a look at Christmases past, from the pages of the Observatory logbook:

1995 "Couldn't ask for a more perfect day than this. Nine degrees, sunny, 10-mph winds and undercast clouds. Almost caught up with summaries and paperwork left by the 'sick' crew. I must say those guys did make an effort at decorating."

1991 "A beautiful day on the Rockpile. Clear, cold, below zero all day. Windy at first, but calming down later. Dinner is turkey with all the fixings. Lots of calls from folks wishing us a Merry Christmas."

1988 "I hope the storm lets up enough to let Santa Claus through. On the night shift, I might even get to see him. Ever wonder if Santa has Doppler radar, or does he still rely on Rudolph?"

1980 "A cold night. Dinner was turkey à la frostbite, and no water to wash it down. Peak gust at 135 mph."

1978 "Santa Claus ahead of schedule. Will stop at Mt. Washington for a snack before heading south. Majority of afternoon spent shoveling snow in the museum. It drifted in through a broken window."

1977 "Christmas on the Rocque Pyle. Al opens his present early (cheat, cheat). White Christmas with eight inches of new snow (the valley gets rain). Nice out now but getting cold fast."

Winter is prime season for search-and-rescue operations. One evening, half an hour after the sun released one last warm ray of light, a frostbitten camper crawled up to the summit in 90-mile-per-hour winds. His face was pale white, like a ghost's, signaling the onset of frostbite. Feeling pity, the summit crew took him in for the night.

The next day, an avalanche bulletin was faxed to the summit, warning of yet another risk to hikers and skiers in the White Mountains: "The John Sherburne Ski Trail is open to the bottom but with a snow bridge crossing the river, so extra caution is advised." Holes in the snow have been known to appear and swallow the unwary.

Frostbite and avalanches are two dangers that await hikers and skiers who come to admire the stark beauty of the mountains in winter. But few people expect the snow to give way underfoot and swallow them up. Mount Washington isn't Everest, after all. On a pleasant winter day (if there ever truly is such a thing), the challenge of conquering Mount Washington's summit is relatively small; just park your car at the Pinkham Notch visitor's center and scramble to the summit in a few hours. But remember: A day that starts with a warm smile from the sun can quickly and unexpectedly turn into an icy snarl.

All in all, Mount Washington is a small mountain, dwarfed by the Himalayas and the Rockies. But climbing it still brings risks, especially in winter. Inexperience and reckless behavior, combined with relatively easy access to the high peaks, is often a deadly mix. Some hikers don't prepare for the possibility of sudden savage skies. More than 140 people have died on Mount Washington and in the nearby Presidential Range since British hiker Frederick Strickland succumbed to hypothermia in 1849.

When Mother Nature growls and swallows the unwary, search-and-rescue teams—including staff from the Observatory, the State Park, the Appalachian Mountain Club, and the Forest Service—must find them and carry them to safety.

"The mountain claims another life today as a man is found expired on the Cog Railway track about 1½ miles from the base," reads one logbook entry. "He was planning a day trip alone up to Lakes [the Lakes of the

Clouds hut] via the Ammonoosuc Trail. Did not come out on time to Fish & Game, and the AMC with helicopter started the search. He had no ice ax, crampons, or overnight gear with him."

Of course, some search-and-rescue operations have happy endings. "We monitored a so-called search-and-rescue one morning," recalls Observer Norm Michaels. "A couple was overdue at Lakes of the Clouds and were last seen in Edmunds Col, on the way over from Mount Madison. Eventually, the [AMC] system figured out they had changed their reservations and decided to stay at Madison. They were 'found' in the bunkhouse."

Wind whisks heat away from any exposed skin, which can make the temperature feel lower than it actually is. Even a soft breeze against your skin can make you feel as if you have suddenly stepped from a refrigerator into a freezer. Exposed skin will freeze solid in less than a minute when the windchill factor (or windchill index) is below -100°, as it often is on Mount Washington. The effect applies only to uncovered skin, which is why ears, noses, and hands are so vulnerable to frostbite. For this reason, staffers on Mount Washington protect themselves with gloves, facemasks, goggles, and balaclavas.

The National Weather Service adopted an undated and improved windchill temperature index in 2001, replacing the formula conceived of by Paul Siple in 1939, which had been in widespread use since 1945. There had always been some controversy about the windchill factor. Siple's formula stops registering a drop in apparent temperature after about 50 mph or so, and in lesser winds probably yields apparent temperatures that are more "extreme" than is really the case. But that's why the old windchill index was so popular with TV weather people. It's much more exciting to say, "The windchill today is minus 80!" than it is to say, "The windchill is minus 35!"

We've learned a lot more about meteorology and how weather affects the human body since 1945, and the new windchill temperature index takes that knowledge and experience into account. Here's a quick comparison of the old and new windchill charts:

Temperature (°F)	50	32	14	-4	-13	-22	-31	-50

At 20 mph, here's how they compare:

Old (1945–2001)	33	7	-19	-44	-57	-70	-83	-110
New (2001–present)	44	20	-4	-27	-39	-51	-63	-88

And now at 40 mph:

Old (1945–2001)	26	-2	-30	-59	-73	-87	-101	-131
New (2001–present)	41	16	-9	-34	-47	-59	-72	-98

LYNNE HOST

METEOROLOGIST SARAH LONG CHECKS THE TEMPERATURE IN THE "THERMOSHACK." SPECIAL "MAX" AND "MIN" THERMOMETERS RECORD THE HIGHEST AND LOWEST TEMPERATURES, AS WELL AS THE CURRENT TEMPERATURE.

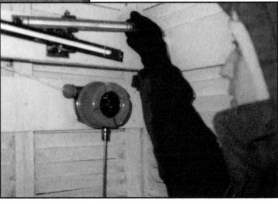

ERIC PINDER

Windchill and frostbite can combine to have a deadly effect. One icy January morning in 1994, the temperature dipped to -15°F, with winds gusting to 65 mph, and according to the forecast, the weather would only get worse.

Ken Rancourt was driving the Observatory's Sno-Cat to the summit, leading a group of eight people on a winter EduTrip. (An EduTrip brings a group of six to ten people to the summit, where members of the Observatory team introduce them to topics such as geology, nature photography, or meteorology.) The participants of that week's trip planned to stay overnight on the highest peak in New England and learn about the worst weather in the world. Little did they realize that they were going to learn more than they ever wanted to know.

They arrived safely on the summit even though winds kicked up, blowing snow and creating whiteout conditions. Then the fun really began. Norm Michaels, shift leader that day, recalled the events in a short essay he wrote for the Observatory's *News Bulletin*:

> Just before dinner, the EduTrippers were ready to experience the high winds and take some photos outside. Several tried to cross the icy roof deck to the northwest railing. But none made it, since the strong, gusty wind knocked them off their feet and slid them along until they reached a wind-sheltered spot from which they could crawl back to the door.
>
> Around 7 p.m. we all sat down for a big turkey dinner. During the meal I took a phone call, a man who wanted to speak to Ken. I turned to the table, but Ken was gone.
>
> "Amid all the noise and jovial conversation at the dinner table," Ken told me later, "I basically heard a noise I didn't like. I thought at first it might be an antenna that had broken loose on the tower and was hanging by a cable, banging against the side of the building. Then I realized it wasn't rhythmic enough for that. I stood up and looked at Ralph and said I didn't like that sound. Let's go upstairs and check it out."
>
> Outside, they found a half-frozen young man named Jeremy, banging on the door. They brought him inside and sat him down in the electronics room. He didn't have much strength left and

he was complaining of the bright lights in the weather room hurting his eyes, which were almost frozen. He was not wearing goggles.

In the kitchen, we were still making merry around the dinner table when an urgent summons came from Ken on the intercom. He had called the hospital, and since it did not look like an evacuation would occur soon, we were advised to start warming [Jeremy's] hands.

The fingerless glove liners had to be cut off. His fingers were porcelain white. At first, we thought he had white gloves on.

Ken—"He was into hypothermia, exhausted and only semi-lucid, but was able to [tell] us over and over something he'd obviously recited to himself all the way over here, and that was the exact location of his friend. There was still another body out there somewhere. I called New Hampshire Fish & Game to alert them to the missing hiker."

Ralph—"We started treatment for hypothermia, the usual stuff—blood pressure checks, oxygen, warm sugary fluids. We moved some portable heaters in and wrapped him up. He was in wicked pain and shivered violently for a little while as his fingers defrosted and his temperature came back up. After a few more calls to the hospital, it was decided to switch to dry heat after the initial thaw."

Early Sunday morning we set a record daily minimum of -42°F, and the winds never abated, averaging over 70 miles per hour all day. Ken made the decision that travel was simply too dangerous, so all our guests settled in for an extended stay. In the meantime, Androscoggin Valley Search and Rescue and Mountain Rescue Services made a monumental effort, attempting to rescue [Jeremy's] friend. Several suffered frostbite, and others called it the hardest rescue they had ever done. Sadly, their efforts were in vain. All they could do was recover the body.

We have learned that Jeremy has lost at least one fingertip. As one [EduTrip] visitor told us, "What you said about the weather was really true. This had been quite an experience."

The people who inhabit the cloudy world above treeline get frequent reminders of how hazardous conditions can be on the high summits. At times, the Mount Washington Auto Road disappears, erased by fog, and it is impossible to tell which way leads to solid ground and which way to a deadly fall, even when one is hiking on that fifteen-foot-wide "highway."

One winter morning during shift change at the Observatory, fog drowned the summit like murky ocean water. A meteorologist hoisted a pack on his shoulders and hiked down from the summit for his week off. Meanwhile, a second crew member was hiking up from below. They had coordinated their hikes and expected to meet each other halfway.

The man coming up started to notice fresh footprints in the snow—footprints that led *down* the road. But he had met no one. All the way up, he saw nothing but fog. When he arrived on the summit and pulled open the Observatory tower door, he was worried. "Where is he? I never saw him going down." Could he have fallen over the edge?

About the same time, the second man emerged from the fog near the base of the clouds and found fresh footprints—going up. Again, he had seen no one. Once he reached the base, he called the summit. "I saw footprints in places but never passed anyone. Did he make it up okay?"

It turned out that the two men had passed each other along the road, perhaps just an arm's reach away. But so thick was the fog and so loud was the wind that they never saw or heard a thing.

"When you walk right by someone and never even notice, that's when you know the fog is thick," one of them remarked later.

Frostbite

Skin is mostly water, so it freezes and expands like ice. A severely frostbitten hand can swell to three times its normal size.

As skin cells start to freeze, the skin turns pale and numb. With superficial frostbite wounds, the skin is cold to the touch but still soft—it hasn't frozen solid. You won't notice any pain yet, but be careful. "You don't want to tug at your ear and have a chunk of it come off in your hand," says a grizzled search-and-rescue man.

Deep frostbite is also free of pain—until you try to rewarm the skin. Then it turns into pure agony.

Safety tips: Bundle up. Minor frostbite (when the skin is still soft) can be treated by warming the frostbitten areas against warm skin. But severe frostbite is dangerous. The worst thing you can do is to refreeze already frostbitten skin. Do not thaw out a severe frostbite wound right away when there is danger of it refreezing—for example, if you are still in the wilderness. Wait until the danger passes, when you return to civilization and have easy access to a hospital.

Part III

Life on the Rockpile

NIN THE CAT SUPERVISES THE WORK OF A WEATHER OBSERVER.

Chapter 7

"The Highest Paying Jobs in New England"

AS NATURE CYCLES THROUGH THE seasons, here on the Rockpile it sometimes feels as if we can experience the best—and worst—of all four seasons every single day. "It's strange to have to worry about pipes freezing in July," reads a logbook entry from July 2, 2001. "The temperature dropped from about 45°F into the 20s in a matter of hours. I was planning to head down in a truck this morning but need to put chains on the tires and am waiting for the 86-mph winds to drop before going outside to do that."

Despite the variability of the weather, each season brings a comfortable routine to the Observatory. In summer, for example, the summit crew and State Park rangers share the peak with a quarter of a million sightseers, hikers, and backpackers. Each morning, the Cog Railway locomotive chugs up the steep slopes like the Little Engine that Could.

Winter brings an entirely new set of responsibilities and expectations. The doors of the State Park building and gift shop are sealed from late October until late May; savage weather soon buries the Cog tracks under hillocks of drifting snow. Winter winds are powerful enough to push snow through cracks in doorways, so the Observatory crew must occasionally shovel snowdrifts *inside* the Mount Washington Museum.

The More Things Change . . .

Times may have changed, but the weather on Mount
Washington hasn't . . . much. A United States Army Signal
Service station housed two to three observers on the summit
in the late 1800s, monitoring the weather. In 1873, a Signal
Service man noted in *their* logbook, "For several weeks we have
experienced considerable difficulty in cutting our way out of
the Depot and letting in daylight through the windows . . . One
drift reaches more than halfway up to the roof."

A RARE LOOK INSIDE THE SIGNAL SERVICE
STATION ON MOUNT WASHINGTON, CIRCA 1873.

As October edges into November and the full force of winter hits the Rockpile, transportation on shift-change day becomes a weekly challenge. Ridges of snow and layers of ice cause the Observatory's van to slip and slide. Soon a four-wheel-drive truck with chains on its tires is the only safe means of reaching the peak. By late December, not even this big vehicle can negotiate the growing snowdrifts.

After that point, a tank-like Bombardier snow tractor is used to plow a path to the summit, a trip that lasts an hour and a half even in the best of circumstances. In foul weather, when low clouds and rime obscure visibility, and hills of snow bury the snow tractor's route up the Mount Washington Auto Road, the 7.6-mile journey can take four hours or even more.

Sometimes the Bombardier never makes it to the summit at all. After struggling through zero visibility and 100-mph winds for four straight hours and still getting only halfway up the mountain, the driver may decide that the safest choice is to turn back and try again tomorrow.

Radio chatter between the Bombardier driver and the summit crew can be very entertaining on shift-change day. "I can't see a thing!" said driver Chris Uggerholt, stuck on the five-mile grade on a questionable shift-change day. "What's the weather doing up there now?"

The crew on the summit was eager to go down. You could hear it in their voices. They'd been working eight days straight and were ready to return to the valley, do their laundry, and catch up on sleep. If the snow tractor couldn't make it, they'd have to work an extra day and have one less day off. The last thing they wanted is for the Bombardier to turn around. So the observer on the summit replied in an increasingly desperate voice, "The wind's still 130 mph, visibility's about fifty feet, but . . . but . . . but I think it's getting better! Is that a hint of sun? I think it might be. The wind's down to 128 now. Yep, conditions are definitely improving."

My shiftmates and I were once stuck on the summit for two extra days due to foul weather. By the tenth day, we were all out of laundry but cheerfully resigned to our fate. We played a lot of Scrabble on the last day.

Only a handful of observers (and, until 2002, two technicians at the WMTW-TV transmitter building) stay on the summit through the entire winter. Supplies such as fresh food are brought up by snow tractor each Wednesday, weather permitting. Tap water for showers and washing dishes is stored in giant holding tanks, located in a deep corner of the Sherman Adams Summit Building.

Deep winter on the Rockpile is a lonelier, quieter time. In summer, by comparison, dozens of park rangers, Cog Railway engineers, Auto Road drivers, and Appalachian Mountain Club guides also work on the mountain. More than 250,000 visitors and sightseers crowd the slopes and summit each year, mostly on sunny summer weekends.

As the seasons change, so too does life at the top.

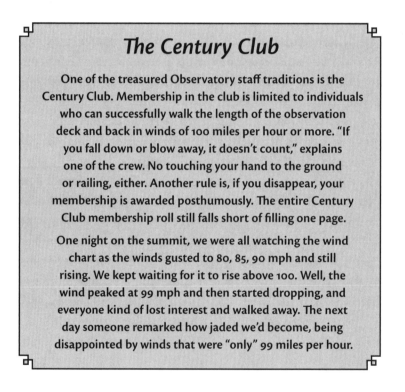

The Century Club

One of the treasured Observatory staff traditions is the Century Club. Membership in the club is limited to individuals who can successfully walk the length of the observation deck and back in winds of 100 miles per hour or more. "If you fall down or blow away, it doesn't count," explains one of the crew. No touching your hand to the ground or railing, either. Another rule is, if you disappear, your membership is awarded posthumously. The entire Century Club membership roll still falls short of filling one page.

One night on the summit, we were all watching the wind chart as the winds gusted to 80, 85, 90 mph and still rising. We kept waiting for it to rise above 100. Well, the wind peaked at 99 mph and then started dropping, and everyone kind of lost interest and walked away. The next day someone remarked how jaded we'd become, being disappointed by winds that were "only" 99 miles per hour.

"There's no such thing as bad weather, only inappropriate dress," is a commonly heard aphorism on Mount Washington. It's a longwinded way of saying "bundle up before you freeze." Weather observers on the summit pile on layers of clothing before going outside to de-ice or do

THERE IS ALWAYS MORE SNOW TO SHOVEL.

an hourly "ob." Stacey Kawecki describes her layers: "Long johns, fleece pants, snow pants, wool socks, snow boots, a sweater, down jacket, Gore-Tex shell, face mask, mittens, goggles, hat." She adds, "I wear two hats, because if I don't, they blow off my head."

It's a typical winter night, and a cold front is expected to pass through New Hampshire and Maine. On weather maps, a cold front is drawn, appropriately enough, as a spiky blue line, as if it were ready to stab the ground with its spears of cold wind.

Already the wind howls. When wind roars across the observation deck at 100 miles per hour, it's easy to imagine a great beast hunched outside the door, claws groping and digging around the tower, trying to rip the basement out by the roots.

Downstairs in the Observatory, we hear wind hammering at the concrete walls. Each gust hisses through cracks in the window casings, spitting snow inside the building. Night Observer Lynne Host discovers a window slightly ajar, but to close it she must step over a mound of fresh snow. "Someone's going to have to shovel that up," she says, waving an arm at a snowdrift sloping out of the bunkroom nearest the kitchen.

How often do you have to shovel up a snowdrift in your kitchen? Once or twice a year, if you are lucky enough to live on Mount Washington. Meteorologist Mark Ross-Parent recalls a time when he headed down to the valley for six days, closing his bunkroom door behind him. No one in the upcoming crew needed to use his room, so the door stayed closed—until the end of the week, when one man thought he heard noises inside the room. He opened the door and found a room packed with snow, a giant ice cube covering beds, dressers, and bunks.

"I remembered I had left the window open a crack, because it was warm," says Ross-Parent. "It took a long time to shovel out. I got a lot of grief for that."

Life at the Top

I step outside to take a weather observation, deep in the fog. The wind presses and prods my skin, stretched taut with cold across my cheekbones. Each gust slaps my face like the misty palm of a ghost who haunts the clouds. The hiss of wind is like the rustle of a million leaves.

The fog cascades across the mountain, a noisy river of air. Waves of mist ripple and churn at my feet. I sometimes think I could hop into a canoe and paddle away on this stream of fast-moving fog. When I look east, turning my head into the breeze, the wind tugs at my ear, pulling me along the trail. I wrench my head back to one side, feel my ear settle back against my skull.

At a hundred miles an hour, clouds hurtle past the mountain. I ponder how Henry David Thoreau described the lands in the clouds.

Thoreau climbed many mountains in New England and soon decided that mountains were "cloud factories." He climbed Mount Washington twice, in 1839 and 1858, but never published a word about New England's highest peak. All that survives to document his two journeys are a few notes scribbled hastily in black ink in his journal.

When he approached the Mount Washington Valley with his brother in 1839, he wrote, "Now we were in a country where inns begin—And we too now began to have our ins and outs." For days, Thoreau "shuddered through that Franconia where the thermometer is spliced for winter use, saw the blue earth heaved into mountain waves from Agiocochook." Later, he "heard the lambs bleat in Bartlett on the mountains late at night." Remarks about sheep appear quite often in his journal, but he says nothing about the mica-schist boulders on Mount Washington or the windy world above treeline.

In 1846, Thoreau made a partial ascent of Katahdin, the tallest mountain in Maine. Like Mount Washington, Katahdin thrusts a wall of naked rock thousands of feet above timberline. Here Thoreau finally recorded his thoughts about the lands above the trees. His description could equally well describe the summit of Mount Washington: "I arrived upon a side-hill, or rather side-mountain, where rocks, gray silent rocks, were the flocks and herds that pastured, chewing a rocky cud at sunset. They looked at me with hard gray eyes, without a bleat or a low. This brought me to the skirt of a cloud, and bounded my walk that night.

" . . . Now and then some small bird of the sparrow family would flit away before me, unable to command its course, like a fragment of the gray rock blown off by the wind." Substitute ravens for sparrows, and Thoreau has just described a familiar scene outside the Observatory weather room window.

Thoreau continues: "I was deep within the hostile ranks of clouds. It was like sitting in a chimney and waiting for the smoke to blow away."

Thoreau fled back to the forest, where a sturdy roof of spruces held back the sky's wrath. Here at the Observatory, we can test ourselves against the 100-mph winds and then quickly retreat indoors. But Thoreau had no bunker-like building in which to hide from the storm. In dying sunlight and by the red embers of his campfire, he wrapped himself in a blanket and scribbled fitfully in his journal. "It reminded me . . . of Atlas, Vulcan, the Cyclops, and Prometheus. Such was the Caucasus and the rock where Prometheus was bound . . . . It was vast, Titanic, and such as man never inhabits."

Things That Go Bump in the Night

A mysterious entity called "The Presence" is said to haunt the summit of Mount Washington. Certain visitors to the summit awaken from chilling dreams. One man staggered out of the six-bunk room and slept on the sofa instead, explaining, "I can't sleep in there. Someone was murdered there."

When asked to explain (we checked for bodies first!), the man said he had just had the most vivid dream set in the 1800s. Long ago, he swore, someone had been killed on the rocks at the exact spot where that particular bunkroom now stands.

Ghost stories like that may be good fun around the dinner table in the company of friends, but the summit building can be a spooky, lonely place when you're the only one awake. "There *is* definitely something to it when those night observers talk about how eerie it can be," says Stacey Kawecki. Normally she works the day shift but filled in on the night shift one week in January 2007. While collecting the precipitation can at half past midnight, she walked alone through the empty rotunda. "I could hear every footstep, and unable to help myself, I glanced at the painted picture of Lizzie Bourne." Lizzie Bourne died of exposure on the summit in 1898. In the Observer Comments, Stacey wrote, "My imagination started to run away. I felt butterflies; not the happy, excited kind." Outside,

ERIC PINDER

**THE SHERMAN ADAMS SUMMIT BUILDING
CREAKS AND MOANS IN THE WINTER.**

the generator was off, deepening the silence. "As I rounded the corner of the building and became exposed to the winds, I heard a howling noise, jumped, and frantically searched for the source. After taking a deep breath, I realized it was the wind moving over the opening on the precip can. Throw murky fog into the mix, and those butterflies in my stomach quickly turned to jumping beans doing the polka." She returned to the brightly lit weather room with a sense of relief.

Mark Ross-Parent remembers working the night shift. He, too, had to change the precip can, and his footsteps echoed down the long corridor. The windows were dark; the long rows of empty picnic tables cast eerie shadows. All was silent and still, except for one . . . *thing*. As Mark walked past the gift shop, he spotted a row of tiny toy trolls dangling from the shelf. Nine of them hung in a row, grinning their eerie, plastic grins.

All were motionless, except for the one in the center. That one was swaying back and forth, the only thing moving in the entire Sherman Adams building. Mark froze. The troll continued to grin at Mark, swaying back and forth in the midst of its motionless companions.

The wind howled. The evil toy troll swung side to side like the pendulum of a clock. Tick, tick, tick.

"I finally decided to confront my worst fear," says Mark. He walked over to the troll and found a heat vent below the shelf, blowing warm air up toward the display case. The current was enough to make the toy sway back and forth.

Sawdust from the Blog
December 27, 2007

"Between the calm winds and no running generators, it is eerily silent—so silent that one can hear the whisper of snow falling to the ground (and not smacking into the windows)."

EVERY SIX HOURS, WEATHER OBSERVERS WALK
OUTDOORS TO CHANGE THE PRECIPITATION CAN. THEN
THEY MEASURE THE SNOWFALL OR RAINFALL IN THE
WARMTH AND SAFETY OF THE WEATHER ROOM.

I, too, heard my share of mysterious creaking noises and bumps in the night during my seven years on Mount Washington. But I never saw any ghosts. On most weeks, I worked the day shift. On the occasions I worked the night shift, I'd be extremely tired and irritable after midnight. I wasn't scared of any ghosts. They were scared of me.

If any ghosts had shown up, my reaction probably would've been a grumpy, "Yeah? What do *you* want?"

There was only one night I was really, truly scared. I still remember it vividly. After dinner, the crew had watched an old *Star Trek* episode, during which the spaceship crew was having mysterious nightmares. At one point, the ship's doctor was in a morgue, surrounded by bodies on carts, all covered in sheets. She suddenly tensed, and when she turned around . . . the bodies are all sitting up, still covered in sheets.

That creepy image lingered in my mind as I started the night shift that week, instead of my usual day shift. Around 0330 EST, ice was accumulating, and I needed to climb up the tower and de-ice the instruments. A small room exists about halfway up the tower. It's called the Cold Room. You climb up a ladder through a hole in the floor. Then you must step off onto the floor, turn, and go to another ladder to the top. But I never got that far.

Partway up the ladder, as my head poked up into the Cold Room, I froze. The haunting image from the TV show flashed back in my mind. Suddenly I knew, beyond a doubt, that if I turned around and looked at the Cold Room, dead bodes in sheets would be sitting upright behind me. I clung to the ladder till my fingers went white. This was crazy, I thought. The wind shrieked—the walls creaked. Finally, I forced myself to look. And, of course, there was nothing there. Still, I was glad to get back downstairs. Nin purred on the seat next to me, a reassuring presence.

Chapter 8

Alpine Animals

IS THE ABOMINABLE SNOWMAN REAL? Probably not. Yeti could be.

With freezing fog, blinding whiteout conditions, and drifting snow to quickly cover over any giant footprints, who's to say an oversized, furry, two-footed mammal doesn't lurk somewhere on the summit of Mount Washington? Or perhaps that creature we saw was just one of the crew after going without shaving for eight days.

The existence of Yeti would be a funny explanation for some of the mysterious thumps and knocking noises we hear in the Sherman Adams summit building, which usually get attributed to wind or the creaking of the walls. I've never seen any Yeti on Mount Washington (though I've inflicted my Yeti pun on visitors hundreds of times). But plenty of other strange animals (and people) populate the summit.

Would you believe that a beaver once hiked to the summit? I didn't believe it either. "What's all the commotion?" I asked one of the rangers on a summer day in 1995. Tourists in the Sherman Adams Summit Building were chatting excitedly about something they'd just seen.

"There's a beaver in the upper parking lot," said the ranger.

I laughed. "Yeah, right. What's really going on?"

"It's a beaver. Honest."

When I walked down to see for myself, the beaver was just starting to leave, waddling back down the Auto Road. He hadn't quite made it to the top—he stopped and turned around in the upper parking lot, where a long, steep set of stairs leads up to the summit. Why it decided to climb Mount Washington in the first place, we'll never know. That's a long hike on those little, stubby legs.

You never know what you'll encounter on Mount Washington. Video footage of a bear loping across the boulders near the Cog tracks provides proof of just how fast they can run. Hikers know how difficult it is to scramble over sharp rocks and giant boulders, but this bear made the trek look effortless. The bear appeared to almost glide over the boulders. "Never try to outrun a bear" is good advice.

"There's a bear eating blueberries down in the Alpine Garden!" announced a summit volunteer one afternoon, as she returned from a late summer hike. The Alpine Garden lies about a mile or so down the trail. I had been working the morning shift since 4 a.m. and needed a break, so I grabbed a pail and walked down the trail to see for myself. The bear, alas, wandered back below treeline before I reached the Alpine Garden. But the bear left behind enough blueberries for muffins and pancakes the next morning.

Given how fast bears run and how fond they are of berries, I'm probably lucky we didn't cross paths while I was toting a pail of blueberries back to the Observatory.

SOMETIMES
BEARS ARE
CLOSER THAN
YOU THINK.

Moose wander up to the summit on rare occasions. The tragic story of Millie the Moose recounts one of the more memorable visits by a member of the species *Alces alces*. A noise—*clump, clump, clump*—alerted the summit crew that something large and heavy was walking on the roof. "That sounds like a moose on the observation deck!" said one of the crew, a photographer. He rushed out the front door of the Sherman Adams building to get a picture.

At the time, a staircase led up to the observation deck from the front door of the summit building, instead of the paved ramp walkway that exists today. Fog swirled about the summit that day, as usual. The moose and the man almost collided before they saw or heard each other. As the man ran up the staircase, he met the moose coming down.

Startled, the moose panicked, backed up, did a lap around the observation deck, then jumped over the railing on the other side. And that was the end of Millie the Moose. The Observatory crew notified Fish & Game, which apparently told the crew that it would be a shame to let all that moose meat go to waste. So Millie remained a presence on the summit, at least in the Observatory freezer, for many months to come.

"I regret I missed the visit of Millie the Moose," says Peter Crane, "though I did have the opportunity to enjoy her company in other ways—out of the freezer."

Sawdust from the Log
Summer 1993

"Big news today is the moose, sighted early afternoon near the lower parking lot, hanging out on a patch of sedge. He was still there at dark. I guess this is moose 3 for the season. Let's hope he's a survivor, though I suppose there are some who'd like to see him in the freezer."

Once I watched a fox use a snowdrift as a natural freezer. The fox carried some summit leftovers—chicken scraps—off of Raven Rock and buried it all in the snow, saving it for later. But as soon as the fox trotted away, a clever raven swooped down and stole all the food.

An entire family of foxes prowls the summit cone. In summer, the foxes know the tourist schedule. As the last car disappears around the bend below Homestretch on the Auto Road, we'll often see the fox trotting up over the boulders to see what yummy scraps the tourists have left behind.

Sawdust from the Log
Summer 1996

"We've been in the fog pretty much all day, except for an hour right around sunset, which featured some nice colors, beautiful clouds, and a double rainbow on the horizon. Even the fox came out on the observation deck to admire the view. She was very tame and came within ten feet of me, staring at me with inquisitive, intelligent-looking eyes."

Sawdust from the Log
Summer 1994

"Hip hip hooray! The fog's gone away. Low clouds spill over the northern Presidentials and produce a beautiful dark-red sunset. A spectacular star show and ninety-mile visibility entertain us in the evening. Even the fox stops by for a visit."

A SUMMIT FOX ENJOYS A NAP.

The first "wild" animal I encountered on the summit was neither a fox nor a bear nor a moose. Instead, it was a chubby orange beast named Jasper. You won't find this animal listed in any zoology books; he was known to only a few. He lurked in his lair deep below ground, in the living quarters of the Observatory.

I first met Jasper the cat on a chilly evening when westerly winds were whipping across the summit at seventy miles per hour. I stood alone on the mountaintop and watched a dark fist of cloud punch slowly toward the peaks, beaching itself on the rocks. Gray mist splashed on the boulders like ocean spray. As I stumbled through the fog, bullets of hail nipped at my face, and the hood of my jacket flapped like a sail. With each strong gust, the precipitation can I was carrying squirmed in my arms like an angry cat.

I encountered a truly angry cat back in the shelter of the Observatory. Jasper was not a happy animal when I rudely walked in from the cold and picked him up; I even had the nerve to try to pet him. He struggled in my arms until I let him go but graciously accepted a bowl of milk as a peace offering. He even begged pitifully for a second peace offering two minutes later.

"Is Jasper an outdoor cat?" I wondered aloud.

One of my co-workers laughed. "I wouldn't say that. The only door Jasper waits in front of is the refrigerator's."

For fourteen years, Jasper survived inside the warm belly of the Mount Washington Observatory while sleet and hail battered the windowpanes and hurricane-force winds rattled the walls. Outside, sheets of ice rain have shattered on the rocks like glass, but a snoozing Jasper purred through it all.

Like most cats, Jasper was a hunter. One night, he trotted off into the twilight and jogged back with a mouse tucked between his jaws. He deposited his prize in the doorway and ran back for more. By night's end, a row of rodents lay scattered across the observation deck, sorted by size. Everyone was surprised.

"He was stacking them up like cordwood," announced one early riser. We expected the Environmental Protection Agency to show up any minute to declare the American house mouse an endangered species.

What's so odd about an orange tabby cat who lives on a mountain and likes to eat asparagus? In Jasper's case, quite a bit. He often fled in terror from children but tolerated adults, so long as they held him upside down (he hated being held right-side up) and so long as they put plenty of milk in his drinking bowl.

For more than a decade, a traumatized Jasper played second fiddle to Inga, the famous calico cat with frosty whiskers. Inga was always the teacher's pet, the spoiled child. A darling of the media, she was "interviewed" by *Cat Fancy* magazine while a jealous Jasper sulked in obscurity.

A picture of an icy Inga is still printed on T-shirts, posters, postcards, and refrigerator magnets that are sold each summer in the Mount Washington Museum gift shop. When Inga passed away in 1993 at age nineteen, her estate generously donated all proceeds from her modeling career to the Observatory.

Sadly, Jasper enjoyed no such notoriety. While thousands of Inga postcards were (and still are) shipped to mailboxes all across the continent, poor Jasper lurked in the shadows, far from the public eye. Even worse, a new nemesis named Nin appeared on the scene in 1996, just

AL OXTON / MOUNT WASHINGTON OBSERVATORY

ICY INGA'S FAMOUS PORTRAIT.

when Jasper finally thought he had the summit to himself. (Rumors to the contrary, Nin's name is not short for *nincompoop*—though it should be!) Nin poses for the cameras and purrs in the arms of visiting journalists. He liked to rob Jasper's food bowl when the older cat wasn't looking.

Jasper, patient as always, endured. The only legacy of this big, shy, but basically friendly cat is likely to be a clump of orange furballs left behind on the living room rug

Cats have always lived at the Observatory, starting with Tikky the tailless manx in 1932. Tikky can be seen as a dark blob tucked under the arm of Sal Pagliuca in the famous photo of the original Observatory crew in 1932 (page 20). But Inga was the first truly "famous" cat, and the photograph of her covered in rime continues to sell to this day.

Poor Jasper was sick and living in the valley when Nin first came to the summit in 1996. So Nin had the summit to himself at first, at least as far as other cats were concerned. A few months later, Jasper came back. At first, Nin was terrified of this big orange intruder. For almost a week, Nin refused to go downstairs where Jasper was lurking. We had to bring up a food bowl to the weather room. If Jasper wandered up into the weather room, Nin would bolt. But eventually, they got used to each other. Sadly, our two-cat summit team didn't last long. Jasper's health took a turn for the worse and he retired again to the valley before the next winter set in. He died in 1997.

Sawdust from the Log
August 14, 1988

"Heavy rain and spectacular t-storms kept tourism low. Few visitors, except for the toad who hopped inside."

August 15, 1988

"That crazy toad was found this evening in the bottom of the tower. The west wind has blown in an inch or so of rain to make it just right for a toad. On Mount Washington? We took plenty of pictures so the other shift would believe us."

Sawdust from the Blog
September 21, 2001

"Well, our friend the owl, Hedwig, as we have decided to call her (although she is a bard owl, and not at all white) has stayed with us all day. She was still perched just outside the Tip Top House when I went out to get the precipitation can this evening."

Nin picked up where Inga left off as the summit's celebrity cat. For more than a decade, Nin served as the summit's Chief Host, Weather Room Supervisor (he loved to curl up on a flat computer that overlooked the desk where observers were working), and self-appointed tester of laps.

UNLIKE SHY JASPER, NIN KNOWS
HOW TO WORK THE CROWDS.

Nin could always be counted on to find the exact center of attention. One winter day, I was giving a slide presentation for a group of EduTrip participants. Ten pairs of eyes focused on the screen, so of course that's where Nin wanted to be. I was about to explain how glaciers had carved U-shaped valleys into the mountainside when suddenly, the giant silhouette of a cat blocked the screen, casting a shadow over the picture of Tuckerman Ravine. Nin had hopped up onto the table and stood directly in front of the projector light. Everyone laughed.

Nin liked to follow us around during "obs," the hourly weather observations. Sometimes, he would follow me right up into the tower. A long metal ladder leads up to the Cold Room, with a frightening fall beneath it. I used to worry about Nin coming back down that ladder, but somehow he managed it, hopping from rung to rung with feline dexterity.

Nin "retired" from the summit the day after Christmas in 2007 and now lives in the valley home of two Mount Washington State Park rangers. "He loves to spend time outside on their deck, lying in the sun," says Observer Brian Clark. "Because of his light fur color, he has to have sunscreen put on his ears." After all those years of living in the fog, perhaps a warm, sunny retirement home in the valley is just what Nin deserves.

NIN AT WORK.

The current cat, Marty, came to the summit in January 2008. Whereas Nin had shown up as a stray at the valley home of one of the observers in Putney, Vermont, Marty was discovered at the Conway Area Humane Society's shelter when he was two years old. Pictures of three cats, including Marty, were put up on the Observatory's web site, and the public was invited to vote on which one would be the new summit cat. "I'm not sure how many votes Marty claimed," says Director of Programs Peter Crane. "Perhaps he only won by a whisker" (ouch!).

After more than 8,000 votes were cast, the snow tractor carried Marty to the summit in January 2008. "I let him out of his carrier in the living room just after arrival," recalls Brian Clark. "He was noticeably spooked and tentative at first, but after only half an hour, he was warming up to the crew, rubbing against our legs and purring."

Kyle Paddleford described the new cat's intelligence and fondness for water in the Observer Comments on January 25: "He bats his water dish for fun and knocks over the occasional cup or glass, too. He even loves staring at the water cooler. The way the water bubbles, the way the waves go back and forth, and even the sound of someone filling up their glass just seems to mesmerize him." Marty carefully observed how his human companions pushed a button to get water out of the cooler. "Next thing you know, he was trying to reach the button with his paw!"

Like Nin, Marty is inquisitive and curious but has a different personality. "Marty is not so quick to curl up in just anyone's lap," says Peter Crane. "So when he does curl up in yours, you know that he deliberated and decided you were worth trusting."

"Marty is hot and cold," says summit volunteer Kristy Medeiors. "Snobby or a love bug! He doesn't like to be disturbed while sleeping but loves to get in your room at night to cuddle."

As a young, active, and very frisky cat, Marty presents a challenge to photographers. "He moves around a lot, so he's harder to capture in a suitable pose," Peter says. "In dark environments, his black fur blends right into the background. In brighter environments, his eyes glow almost eerily."

Veteran summit volunteer Steve Moore agrees: "Marty is very black and difficult to see at night when the lights are out except for his bright yellow eyes."

Volunteer Kathy Emerson wrote a note in the Observer Comments about a quiet, starry night in 2008, when she could hear a fox barking outside: "I asked if we should worry about Marty the cat being outside with the fox nearby, and they said no. Marty chases the foxes away. Guess you have to be a pretty bold cat to live in this environment!"

Nin once hiked all the way to Mount Clay and back in 1997, following two of the crew, meowing loudly if they got too far ahead, as if to say, "Wait for me!" But Marty the hiking cat soon outdid his predecessor.

Observer Brian Clark noticed early on that Marty liked to follow him around during the workday. "I began calling him 'my shadow' back in the spring," he says. "Almost every day, he follows me on the morning 'walkaround,' which is when I take a few minutes to walk through the building to make sure everything looks okay and to check certain water, power, and fuel meters." Marty would tag along with Brian during hourly weather observations and even join him if he had to take something down to the Museum in the summer. "The number of people in the main lobby often seems to make him a bit uncomfortable," says Brian, but Marty always went along anyway.

MARTY FOLLOWS IN NIN'S PAWPRINTS. HE
LOVES THE CREW AND LOVES THE SUMMIT.

On September 14, 2008, Brian finished work for the day and decided to hike down to the Lakes of the Clouds hut, which was about to close for the season. "As I was leaving, Marty made it very clear that he wanted to go outside," says Brian. "At the time, I did not worry about him following me." Brian had gone for other hikes that summer without his shadow following him. Not this time, though. Brian described the epic adventure in the Observer Comments: "After Marty gracefully leaped and bounded his way down the trail with me for about two-tenths of a mile, I tried to tell him that I was going a long way and he shouldn't follow me. He didn't listen . . . imagine that."

Brian turned around several times, trying to get Marty to follow him back up to the summit, but Marty just kept on going. He was "gleefully meowing," according to Brian. "I was thoroughly impressed how he was able to follow the trail."

Brian tried to catch Marty a few times, but the cat kept out of arm's reach. "I finally gave up and accepted the fact that Marty was going to join me on the 1.5-mile hike down to Lakes," Brian wrote. He worried a bit about Marty getting tired and thought the cat might want to turn around. But each time he stopped, Marty would stroll right past him down the trail. They continued to hike together, and at times Marty would take the lead.

The sun was setting when they arrived at Lakes of the Clouds. "People were milling about outside and I could hear several exclamations of 'Is that a cat?!' A few people asked me if it was my cat and why I had brought it up here with me. Of course, I explained that it was, sort of, my cat but that I worked for the Observatory and we had come from the summit."

After fifteen minutes, Brian managed to catch Marty and bring him inside the hut. "He was certainly not happy having his exploration cut short, and I have claw marks on my shoulder to prove it," wrote Brian in the Observer Comments.

"Marty was actually very content in the attic of the hut. I brought him some water and leftover turkey that the crew had prepared for the night's dinner. He quickly chowed that down and began purring and butting his head against me, which he often does when he is happy and wants attention."

The dilemma now was how to get Marty back to the summit. "There was no way I was going to just let the little guy go outside and fend for himself," says Brian. "Marty is a very smart cat, and I am reasonably sure that he would make his way back to the summit." But he didn't want to take that chance. He decided to bring Marty back that night, despite the fog and the dark, because the weather was only going to get worse. The forecast called for high winds and rain the next morning.

Brian carried Marty outside and put him down once they were a short distance from the hut. Marty contentedly followed Brian up the trail. "A couple times, he decided he was tired and laid down in the trail," Brian continues in his account of the trip. "I picked him up and gave him a ride for a little bit. Eventually, he would start squirming, I would put him down, and he would continue to follow me."

Marty wears a tiny bell on his collar. "This has earned him the nickname 'Tink-tink' on our shift," says Brian, "and it was very helpful in keeping track of him. The way his eyes glow in the light of my headlamp was also helpful." The trip back took about an hour—not bad at all for a cat. Brian remarked on the Observatory web site that the trip back from Lakes normally takes him 30 to 40 minutes by himself. "Needless to say, Marty was in dire need of a nap when we got back," concludes Brian. The tuckered-out cat instantly fell asleep.

Sawdust from the Log
June 20, 1996

"Nin, the incredible hiking cat, conquers Mount Clay this morning (meower power). Humans Matt and Jake tag along."

**THE SUMMIT CATS LIKE TO SIT IN THE
WINDOW AND WATCH THE RAVENS.**

Invasion of the Flying Squirrels

Alex McKenzie, part of the 1934 Observatory crew that witnessed the world record wind, used to radio up to the summit and chat with the night observer about the weather, until the late 1990s. This was ham radio; anybody could listen in. I had always heard that people liked to tune in to Alex when he called us on the summit—he was an entertaining storyteller—but I never knew how true this was until the flying squirrels invaded.

They were everywhere. Jasper (Nin wasn't on the summit yet) went into hunter mode and caught a few, but he couldn't catch them all. The Sherman Adams Summit Building was infested with flying squirrels. I was the night observer at the time, a rookie. One night at around 3 a.m., when my shift was almost over, I went down to the kitchen to get a bite to eat. Usually, I had the Observatory to myself at that time of night, but a strange figure was standing there in the doorway. It turned out to be one of the people who had been sleeping in the six-bunk room. He looked bleary-eyed and disheveled. "I was sound asleep," he said, "and then a flying squirrel ran right over my face!"

I was telling Alex this story over the radio the next night. He laughed and described a similar experience at the old Observatory. Apparently, this was not the first invasion by flying squirrels.

Seconds after Alex signed off, the Observatory phone rang. I don't remember who it was, but he said, "I just heard you talking with Alex. So, do you need any of those live traps, for all the squirrels?" I guess people really were listening in on the Appalachian Mountain Club hut radios and around the White Mountains.

Sadly, Alex suffered a stroke a year or two later, and the nightly radio call tradition ceased. For a while, John Conover of Blue Hill Observatory would call in each night, while he was dong some snowstake studies on the mountain. And Alex's son volunteered on the summit on more than one occasion. But we all miss Alex.

I sure don't miss those flying squirrels, though. We never did figure out where all the squirrels came from, or where they went. I don't think there's been another summer like that since.

CATS GET MOST OF THE GLORY, BUT DOGS HAVE LIVED ON
THE SUMMIT TOO. NIGHT OBSERVER LYNNE HOST AND
HER DOG, RAINBEAU, HAM IT UP IN THE WEATHER ROOM.

IN PAST DECADES, SLED DOGS PROVIDED AN
ALTERNATIVE TO SNOW TRACTORS.

MANY MT. WASHINGTON OBSERVERS TRAVEL FROM PEAK TO
POLE AND FIND WORK IN ANTARCTICA. MAGNIFICENT VIEWS
OF THE SOUTHERN LIGHTS ARE A PERK OF THE JOB.

Chapter 9

Life at the Bottom—Antarctica

WHY WORK ON A MOUNTAINTOP where you're allowed only one shower a week, the weather is brutal, the pay is minimal, and you have a nonnegligible chance of being struck by lightning? Peter Crane and I once had a very serious conversation on this topic in the Observatory's North Conway office.

"It's a low-pressure job," I declared.

"Sure, most of the time it's a breeze," said Peter.

"Unless someone throws a Cog in the works."

"That's why you always need to put in a peak performance."

"So all of your hard work won't be in vane." The puns and inside jokes flew back and forth while marketing manager and current executive director Scot Henley listened and groaned. Peter probably won the exchange. He's always quick with a pun.

"One thing's for sure," I said, getting in a final bad pun. "If you ever leave the summit, your career will go downhill."

Where *do* people go after leaving the summit? Forecasting and TV meteorology jobs lure away some summit employees. Others head down to the base of the mountain to work for the Appalachian Mountain Club.

One meteorologist, after years of treating his summit shiftmates to delicious homemade bread, opened his own successful bakery. But the most common job change involves a transfer from peak to Pole—from Mount Washington to Antarctica.

"I'm cool because I work at the Pole," says Katie Hess with a laugh. "The world revolves around me. Literally! Ha!" Katie worked for several years as a weather observer on Mount Washington before trading "life at the top" for "life at the bottom." She went on to work for four more years in Antarctica, first as part of the meteorology team and later as winter site manager.

The biggest difference she noticed was the complete lack of wildlife. The geographic pole is hundreds of miles from the coast, so the Pole crew see no penguins, no seals, no blades of grass, not even any mosquitoes. "I've seen a few bugs come in on the lettuce and be kept alive in jars with a leaf of lettuce for everyone to marvel at," says Katie. "That's about the extent of the wildlife here."

At the end of the long, dark winter, she says that tired people start to "see" things like dragonflies, houseflies, "dome dogs," and other shadows of the imagination. "I swear I saw a dog run around the corner in the dome one time," she says with a laugh. A similar phenomenon exists on Mount Washington, where sleep-deprived night observers joke about the existence of "the corner people." You're sure you see somebody in the corner of your eye, but when you turn your head, no one is there.

The Observatory's "Century Club" (those who have walked around the perimeter of the observation deck in sustained winds of 100 mph or greater) has a parallel at South Pole. They call it the 300 Club. Katie Hess explains: "The 300 Club is for those who are lucky enough to see temperatures below -100°F and crazy enough to heat up the sauna to 200°F, strip naked except for shoes or boots, and run outside around the geographic South Pole and back."

Dips below -100°F are rare even at Pole. "Sadly, I am not yet a member," says Katie. In 2008, the lowest temperature all winter was -99.9°F. Back in her first year working on Antarctica, the temperature briefly dropped below -100°F, and eager participants lined up for their chance. By the time they heated up the sauna, the temperature had started to rise into the -90s, "so only one or two people became true members."

Another Mount Washington veteran, Meghan Prentiss, successfully joined the 300 Club in 2002. According to Meghan, joining the Century Club is the more difficult task. "The 300 Club just takes a long spell in the sauna and some courage to step out into the cold. After that, you just keep running and hope the pictures are blurry."

Katie Hess agrees. "The Century Club requires strength, inner courage, and patience," she says. "The difference between 80 mph and 100 mph is dramatic. Only a very few hardy and fiercely strong individuals have made the walk without falling down or using hands."

By contrast, the 300 Club is more embarrassing. "If you're crazy enough to do it, it's not hard at all," says Hess. "The hardship of the 300 Club is getting over the embarrassment of running around naked, drawing up the courage to subject your body to such extremes, and enduring the respiratory irritation and coughing that occurs a few days afterward. Breathing in such dry, cold air essentially burns, or frostbites, the larynx."

Still, everyone wants to tell friends about the experience. According to Katie Hess, "The embarrassment of running naked among co-workers is dulled by the goofy sense of doing something new, something that's been anticipated for months." A cloud of steam forms around each person as they run out of the sauna onto the ice. That steam cloud helps insulate them from the chill, as long as they run fast and the wind isn't blowing. Katie adds, "It's usually dark at the time of year these temperatures occur." That must help blur the pictures.

If a frostbitten larynx doesn't quite render one speechless at the South Pole, a view of the aurora might do the trick, albeit in a more figurative way. "They are at their best in the very cold weather," says Meg Prentiss, "so it's hard to watch for more than a few minutes. The new folks get excited about all the auroras, but the seasoned folks are a little more discriminating. They only go out for the really spectacular ones."

The light show begins at sunset, which lasts longer than you might think. "I once watched the sun set for a week," recalls Mark Ross-Parent, another Observatory veteran who spent three years at Pole.

"Sunset is so gradual here that you get spoiled," Meg Prentiss says. "Constantly changing beautiful color." The sun will slowly orbit the horizon for days before sinking out of sight. "Then when the real darkness sets in, you start to see green searchlights in the sky. They get more spectacular as winter progresses—movement, shapes, swirls, ribbons of pink, yellow, and green."

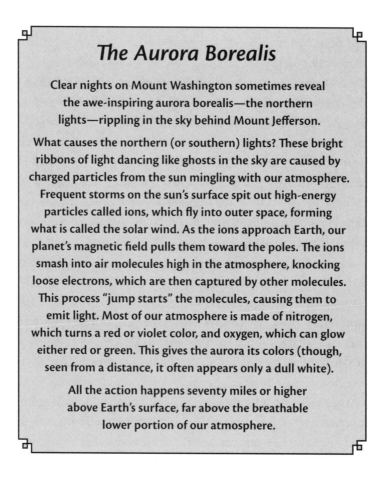

The Aurora Borealis

Clear nights on Mount Washington sometimes reveal the awe-inspiring aurora borealis—the northern lights—rippling in the sky behind Mount Jefferson.

What causes the northern (or southern) lights? These bright ribbons of light dancing like ghosts in the sky are caused by charged particles from the sun mingling with our atmosphere. Frequent storms on the sun's surface spit out high-energy particles called ions, which fly into outer space, forming what is called the solar wind. As the ions approach Earth, our planet's magnetic field pulls them toward the poles. The ions smash into air molecules high in the atmosphere, knocking loose electrons, which are then captured by other molecules. This process "jump starts" the molecules, causing them to emit light. Most of our atmosphere is made of nitrogen, which turns a red or violet color, and oxygen, which can glow either red or green. This gives the aurora its colors (though, seen from a distance, it often appears only a dull white).

All the action happens seventy miles or higher above Earth's surface, far above the breathable lower portion of our atmosphere.

At the South Pole, the aurora is more colorful and the weather much colder than on Mount Washington. Mount Washington boasts stronger winds and more fog, ice, and snowfall. At times, windstorms, once called "Herbies," will kick up a blizzard of blowing snow on Antarctica. "That reminds me of home at the Obs," Katie says. "I miss the autumn leaves the most, and a sweater day walking among the trees, mild breeze, and a nice hike on a three-thousand-footer when all the goofers are gone and it's just quiet. Might sound crazy, but that's a lot of what I miss!"

Despite such differences in the weather, the daily routine of meteorologists at the Observatory and Pole is in many ways the same. The paperwork and METAR coding are familiar sights at either location. Meghan Prentiss adds, "There's also the communal quarters for sleeping and eating, and the fact that someone is trying to sleep at all hours of the day and night. Sometimes it's the same remote feeling you get at the Obs in the middle of the night with the wind blowing. It's funny how the job is so solitary and lonely but the place can be vibrant and fun just because you are all in it together."

Shift change on Mount Washington occurs (weather permitting) once every week. At South Pole, shift change occurs twice a year. "There are really only two seasons, summer and winter," says Katie Hess. In mid-Febuary, the station closes and flights stop. (The temperature is so cold

LIFE IN ANTARCTICA CAN BE AN "IN-TENTS" EXPERIENCE.

MARK ROSS-PARENT

that it can freeze the hydraulics in airplanes. So a plane might be able to land in midwinter, but it wouldn't be able to take off again.) Once the last plane leaves in February, you're stuck there.

"Winter at South Pole dulls the senses," recalls Katie Hess. "Darkness and a rather sterile newly built station dull your vision. Lack of animal and plant growth also dull the sense of smell." Worst of all, she says, "A quiet population of only sixty people that you've been talking to day in and day out for months dulls the hearing." For months, the Pole crew subsists on canned food, dehydrated food, and frozen food. "Even with the best cooking in the world, the absence of fresh produce can dull the sense of taste," Katie laments.

The transition from winter to summer is a hectic one, whether at the Pole or on Mount Washington. The influx of tourists, construction crew, and new workers is sudden and a bit unsettling. "The bosses show up and all the new staff seem like intruders into a previously well-ordered little world," says Meghan Prentiss. The first flight of the season is welcomed, bringing fresh fruits, familiar faces, and news from home. But suddenly the station is abuzz with activity, the population quintuples, and privacy is at a premium. "The hardest part was the change from Pole being 'our' station to all of a sudden, with one flight, being overrun with summer staff."

Tourists visit, too, in the summer, though not nearly as many as on Mount Washington. Distinguished visitors, or "DVs," including Senator John McCain and Senator Susan Collins of Maine, will fly in from McMurdo for souvenirs, photos, and a station tour. Other visitors include a hardy breed of skiers and explorers. "Some people are out to reach Pole first for their country," says Katie Hess, "or to be the youngest, oldest, fastest to reach the Pole overland." People arrive by ski, kite ski, hot-air balloon, helicopter, twin otters, motorcycle vehicles, and once, says Hess, in a "beefed up soccer-mom van."

On Mount Washington, you can quickly distinguish day hikers from Appalachian Trail thru-hikers by smell. The same is true of visitors to the South Pole who have just spent weeks out on the icy plateau. The trek requires more than 40 days of intense labor, according to Hess. "Some of them honestly smell terrible, whether from not showering or from decaying frostbitten skin needing to be treated," she says. "The more competent adventurers look happy and healthy and have done a much better job of managing their hygiene and health." Wealthy individuals pay to fly in by twin otter. "They make it all the way here only to turn around an hour later and never really know what South Pole is . . . "

Saying Goodbye

After a long winter at Pole, Meghan Prentiss remembers waiting for her flight to McMurdo. "I had a hard time saying goodbye to the station, but I was happy to be headed to New Zealand and my first day off in over a year."

What was her reaction to landing in the temperate climate of New Zealand? "Glorious," she says. "Overwhelming. Different smells, new people, animals, insects, flowers, rain, good food. A group of us got so excited when we saw a dog in Christchurch. We were like little kids, so excited to pet it."

Antarctica is basically a continent-sized sensory deprivation chamber, a fact which truly becomes apparent on the way home. The sudden immersion into a temperate climate when the plane lands at Christchurch, New Zealand can be a shocking one.

"I immediately noticed my hair doubling in thickness, I could actually feel it in my scalp," recalls Katie Hess about her first year returning to New Zealand. "Little scabs from cuts and scrapes on my dry, fragile skin were finally healing well. However, the smells were lost on me." She was congested for a week after landing in New Zealand, a side effect of the sterile environment at Pole. "It dulls the immune system to have such a lack of interaction with pollens, pollution, animals, fresh air, and people carrying the latest germs." For many people, what Katie calls "re-entry to the world" can result in allergic reactions, trouble digesting new foods, and sensitivity to sunburn.

The new sights and sounds were amazing enough. "The sight of young children, babies, families, pets, animals, trees, grass, the feel of a warm breeze sitting in the sun, the feel of walking into the ocean waves at the beach—it was so cold but so wet! These things consumed my attention!" The trees were in blossom as the New Zealand summer began. Katie Hess rolled down the windows and went for a drive. "I went swimming, ate oranges, drank milk, tried my first sushi, and thought I was in heaven."

Hearing these tales from so many friends and colleagues at the Observatory, I still feel some regret that I haven't made it to Antarctica—yet. Another longtime Observatory veteran, Peter Crane, has a slightly different take. "I didn't make it to Antarctica but don't harbor deep regret about that," he says. "Six months of subzero darkness is not especially appealing to me. I have a hard enough time trying to grow tomatoes in Bartlett without trying it at Palmer, McMurdo, or the Pole. But if I were to wake up tomorrow and find I was back in my twenties, I would give a short stint on the Ice some consideration."

The Thing

The famous horror movie *The Thing*, set at the South Pole, turns into a comedy when you watch it on the summit of Mount Washington with co-workers who have actually been to the Pole.

At the beginning of the film, an alien monster inhabits the bodies of the German Shepherds at the South Pole station. Except, of course, the Antarctic Treaty of 1969 prohibits domesticated animals on Antarctica. So there wouldn't have been any dogs for the alien invader to possess. More hilarity ensues when the heroes break out the weapons. "I want to know where we kept all those guns and flame-throwers," says Mark Ross-Parent with a laugh.

Antarctica is actually a very good place to find a different kind of invader from outer space. The stark white landscape makes it easy to spot meteorites on the surface. Several Martian meteorites have been collected from Antarctica's ice.

Part IV

Recipes from the Rockpile

LOBSTER IS A RARE TREAT IN THE OBSERVATORY KITCHEN.

Favorites from the Highest Kitchen in New England

IF YOU HAVE EVER WONDERED what people eat on top of the windiest mountain in the world, you're not alone. Visitors to the summit are often shocked to learn that the Observatory boasts a full kitchen and a well-stocked larder.

"We thought you lived in tents!" said one astonished (but well-fed) visitor. He sat down on a couch in the Observatory's small living room and flipped through the pages of an old *National Geographic* magazine while the smell of fresh-baked bread wafted over the counter from the kitchen.

Life on Mount Washington offers all the comforts of home—until you step outside and get whisked off your feet by a hurricane-force breeze. But even when the temperature dips below -30°F, the wind shrieks like a banshee, and buckets of snow drop from the sky, the crew of the Mount Washington Observatory stay close to the stove and cook away their wintertime blues.

Ordering out for pizza is not an option when you are trapped on an icy mountaintop, but just because people live miles away from civilization doesn't mean they can't eat a civilized dinner—or two, if they get the chance.

This section features an assortment of recipes from the highest kitchen in New England. Some meals are old summit favorites, cooked often and eaten with relish. Others are family recipes contributed by Observatory members, volunteers, and staff. And still others, I discovered written in sloppy handwriting on faded yellow pages in the "blue box" that sits on top of the Observatory refrigerator. The blue box has been around so long that its origins are forgotten, lost in the proverbial mists of time.

A recipe is only as good as the cook who makes it. Two people, starting with the same set of ingredients, can come up with entirely different results. Most Observatory meals are delicious and quickly devoured, but others end up as breakfast for the birds on Raven Rock.

To encourage cooking skills among the crew, the Observatory has a tradition of culinary awards. For example, the "Rookie Cookie Award" goes to the newcomer on the staff who makes a better-than-expected meal for the rest of the crew.

"I never won the Rookie Cookie Award my first year on the Rockpile," admits senior Observer Norm Michaels. "Cooking was as much on-the-job training for me as were the daily weather observations. One night, I made something sort of like a chili. Since my shiftmates liked spicy food, I added a lot of pepper. To be color consistent, I chose red pepper. Sadly, at the time, I didn't know the difference in heat between red pepper and black pepper. The result was so hot I thought we would all die. I had to serve ice cream with the main dish, and we still burned out our insides."

NORM MICHAELS
IN NEED OF SOME
OF HIS OWN
SPICY CHILE.

Nowadays, not much has changed. (Well, perhaps Norm's cooking has improved a bit. As a recent entry in the logbook notes: "Chief Observer Norm becomes Chef Observer Norm as he cooks up tonight's dinner: *pizza de resistance!*") Without a doubt, the crew still likes spicy food, as a glance at some of these recipes reveals.

The number of guests on the summit has increased in the last decade, and Observatory volunteers enthusiastically share the eight-day workweek with the crew and take over most of the cooking duties.

"Since I can't afford a cruise to Antarctica, I thought volunteering at the top of Mount Washington might be the next best thing," wrote volunteer Kathy Emerson on the Observatory web page. When she arrived in late August, the temperature was just below freezing, with winds blowing 50 mph. "I loved it!" says Kathy. "Talk about exhilarating!" She soon got used to the summit's quirks. "Coping with an oven that has a mind of its own ('What? 250° isn't hot enough? Okay, I'll go up to 475° and see how you like that!'), trying not to breathe the smoke of the cute little historic Cog railway train as it chugs past, missing my dog (she'd love this place!), and getting laughed at by the tourists when I'm wearing my nifty fleece hat with the ear flaps (and they're freezing in their shorts) are all things I've learned to live with up here," she says.

Except for the one nameless volunteer who burned dinner badly enough to set off the fire alarms in the Sherman Adams building for the first time in memory, all of our volunteer cooks thrive in their new environment. (Smoke billowed up the stairs into the weather room that night; it was so bad, you would have thought the Cog locomotive was in the Observatory living room. The night observer ended up making grilled cheese sandwiches for everyone.) Volunteers not only provide tasty treats, they free up valuable time for the summit staff. It's hard to keep track of the weather and rescue lost hikers if you're also cooking a turkey dinner for fifteen.

"To cook for nonpicky people who like to eat is a gift, and the bonuses are just heaped on top of that," said volunteer chef Mary Webber in the summer of 2006. "Hanging out in the weather room watching the most variable, dangerous, and gorgeous weather in the world" was just part of

**AFTER A HARD DAY'S WORK, A SUMMIT VOLUNTEER
ENJOYS A SPECTACULAR SUNSET WITH NIN.**

the appeal. She went on to say, "To look down into the valley in a clear night and see magical looking villages, to go outside and oh-so-briefly experience windchills in the single digits while at the base of the Auto Road, it's in the 60s—these things are priceless!"

Seasonal Favorites

When it comes to food, we have seasonal favorites, which is perhaps only appropriate for people whose lives are so oriented to weather. For example, spring is the season to enjoy Spring Thaw Soup (page 131) and Alpine Salad (page 137).

Since snowflakes occasionally fall on Mount Washington in the middle of summer, a Christmas dinner on the Fourth of July is not entirely out of the question. Many of our summertime favorites are actually appropriate for any season. These include Gourmet Deep Dish Pizza (page 158), Guadalajara Night Chili (page 148), Sopaipillas (page 179), and Blueberry Streusel Cake (page 171).

Popular recipes for the fall season include Pumpkin Pie (page 170) and Cheese & Wheat Beer Bread (page 127). In winter, the idea is to stay warm, and meals cooked on the mountaintop live up to that ambition. "Strange hamburger/pepper/cheese/onion glop for dinner tonight," notes the logbook in December 1988. Fortunately, aside from that infamous "glop," winter brings in such favorite dishes as Kerosene Rice & Beans (page 164) and Sticky Buns (page 177).

A note about "low-altitude directions." If you have ever seen a "high-altitude alternative recipe" on a box of brownies, you know that changes in elevation and air pressure can have an effect on cooking. Most readers of this book probably live close to sea level, thousands of feet below Mount Washington's summit. For your convenience, recipes in this book are designed for "low altitude" kitchens.

Why mention this? Simply because water boils at a lower temperature at higher elevations, and that affects the cooking time for certain recipes. On Mount Washington, water boils at 202°F instead of the standard 212°.

Air pressure is much lower on the summit, at 6,288 feet, than at sea level. (Peer pressure is higher, though: "Come on! Stop working! Let's all go watch the lightning storm. Everybody's going.") On the mountain, average atmospheric pressure is 23.66 inches, compared with about 29.92 along the coast of Maine. Air on Mount Washington is also about 18 percent thinner than at sea level. (Crew members on Mount Washington are about 18 percent thicker than at sea level, particularly around the waistline, at least if they indulge in too much banana bread and pumpkin pie.) All the billions of air molecules in the atmosphere—200 miles of air—press down on lower air molecules to keep them snug against Earth's surface. That's why air gets thinner the higher you go.

Unfortunately, the subarctic soil also gets thinner. Blizzard-like conditions discourage frequent trips to the grocery store, and chilly winds pretty much wreak havoc on anyone's attempts at gardening. So fresh fruits and vegetables are a seldom-seen luxury. The observatory stocks its pantry with an abundance of canned and frozen items, and the recipes reflect this fact.

In valley kitchens, feel free to substitute fresh produce!

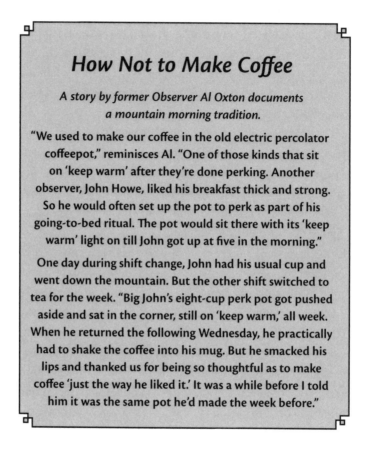

How Not to Make Coffee

*A story by former Observer Al Oxton documents
a mountain morning tradition.*

"We used to make our coffee in the old electric percolator coffeepot," reminisces Al. "One of those kinds that sit on 'keep warm' after they're done perking. Another observer, John Howe, liked his breakfast thick and strong. So he would often set up the pot to perk as part of his going-to-bed ritual. The pot would sit there with its 'keep warm' light on till John got up at five in the morning."

One day during shift change, John had his usual cup and went down the mountain. But the other shift switched to tea for the week. "Big John's eight-cup perk pot got pushed aside and sat in the corner, still on 'keep warm,' all week. When he returned the following Wednesday, he practically had to shake the coffee into his mug. But he smacked his lips and thanked us for being so thoughtful as to make coffee 'just the way he liked it.' It was a while before I told him it was the same pot he'd made the week before."

For a list of recipes, see page viii.

Appetizers, Snacks, Beverages, and Breakfast Treats

Peak-Performance Deviled Eggs

◇◇◇

Contributed by Ken Rancourt

12 eggs
1 heaping tbsp Gulden's brown mustard
2 tbsp mayonnaise
5 oz prepared horseradish (drain and save juice)
2 to 3 tsp ground cayenne pepper (optional)
sugar (optional)
paprika

Hard boil the eggs and let them cool. Peel them, cut them in half lengthwise, and remove yolks. Chop yolks and mix them with mustard, mayonnaise, and horseradish.

Next, cover the mixture with cayenne pepper until it is red all over (omit this step for milder eggs). Generally, use 2 to 3 teaspoons of cayenne pepper, to taste. (Expect an initial jolt from the horseradish, but the real goal is for a slow rise of the heat from the cayenne to develop at the rear of the palate, spreading forward on your tongue to the rest of your mouth.) If you use the correct mixture, the cayenne should not be bitter. A dash of sugar will reduce the bitter taste of too much cayenne.

Finally, stuff the eggs with the yolk/mustard/cayenne mixture. If the mixture is too dry, add a little horseradish juice. Sprinkle with paprika to color the tops.

Granola for Hikers
◇◇◇◇◇◇◇◇◇◇◇◇◇◇◇◇◇◇◇◇◇◇◇◇◇
Contributed by Meredith Piotrow

> 4 cups regular rolled oats (not quick oats)
> 1 cup wheat germ
> ½ cup vegetable oil
> ½ cup honey
> 1 tsp vanilla
> ½ cup grated coconut (optional)
> 1 cup sunflower seeds (optional)
> 1 ½ cups Soya flakes (optional)
> raisins (optional)

Mix ingredients together in a large bowl. If using raisins, add them after baking. Spread onto cookie sheets and bake at 250° to 300°, stirring regularly. When oats are brown and crispy, remove from oven and cool. Store cooled granola in plastic bags or containers with lids.

Orographic Omelet
◇◇◇◇◇◇◇◇◇◇◇◇◇◇◇◇◇◇◇◇◇◇◇◇◇
Contributed by Meredith Piotrow

> 1 ½ tbsp butter
> 4 eggs
> 4 tbsp milk
> paprika
> oregano
> basil
> salt
> ½ cup grated cheese (any kind)
> cooked sausage, ham, or bacon (optional)
> tomatoes, diced (optional)

onions, diced and sautéed (optional)
mushrooms, diced and sautéed (optional)
(Note: total quantity of filling should be
   about ½ to ¾ cup)

Melt butter in frying pan at medium heat. Be sure to spread butter so that it covers the entire pan. In a bowl, mix together eggs, milk, and seasonings to taste. Pour mixture into pan. Run a spatula around the outer edge of the omelet to make sure it isn't sticking or burning.

When egg mixture becomes almost firm, add your choice of grated cheese. Precooked sausage, ham or bacon may also be added. Diced tomatoes, sautéed onions, and sautéed mushrooms are also a nice touch.

When the mixture is entirely firm (not runny), flip half the omelet back onto itself to form a half-moon. Serve hot. Will feed two people, or one Yeti.

Mount Clay Cakers (spiced pancakes)

Contributed by Chris Uggerholt; originally published in The Breakfast Cookbook: Favorite Recipes from America's Bed & Breakfast Inns, *Winters Publishing, 1990.*

1 ¼ cups flour
⅛ cup sugar
1 tsp baking powder
½ tsp baking soda
½ tsp cinnamon
¼ tsp nutmeg
¼ tsp salt
1 egg
1 ¼ cups buttermilk
2 tbsp oil
sliced bananas
butter (whipped)
maple syrup (warmed)

In a large mixing bowl, stir together dry ingredients. In a separate bowl, mix together egg, buttermilk, and oil. Add the liquid to the dry ingredients (push down to make a "well" in the flour mixture before pouring), and stir until blended.

Spoon ¼ cup of butter onto a hot griddle or skillet for each pancake. Flip pancake over once the edges become dry. Serve with sliced bananas, whipped butter, and warm maple syrup.

"CUMULUS BITUMINOUS" IS A COMMONLY
SEEN CLOUD IN THE SUMMER.

Breads, Rolls, and Muffins

Cheese & Wheat Beer Bread

◇◇◇◇◇◇◇◇◇◇◇◇◇◇◇◇◇◇◇◇◇◇◇◇◇◇◇◇◇◇◇◇◇◇

Contributed by Lynne Host

    1 ½ cups beer (a hearty German beer works best)
    ⅔ cup water
    ½ cup olive oil
    1 ½ cups whole wheat flour
    4 to 5 cups white flour
    ½ cup sugar
    ½ cup oatmeal
    1 tsp salt
    2 packages yeast
    1 egg
    2 cups sharp cheddar cheese

Pour beer, water, and olive oil into a saucepan and heat until warm (about 120°F). Next, in a large bowl, combine the warm liquid with whole wheat flour and one cup white flour, plus sugar, oats, salt, yeast, and egg. Beat for 2 minutes.

Next, stir in the remaining white flour by hand. On a well-floured surface, knead the dough until smooth and elastic. Place in a greased bowl and cover; let the dough rise until it doubles in size (1 to 1 ½ hours). While dough is rising, shred 2 cups of cheddar cheese and set aside.

Punch down the risen dough and divide in half. Work one cup of shredded cheese into each half. Finally, shape into 2 loaves and put into well-greased 9-by-5-inch loaf pans. Cover and let rise again 40 to 60 minutes.

Heat oven to 350° and bake for 40 to 50 minutes. Be sure to remove the bread from the pans immediately.

Fake Corn Bread
◇◇◇◇◇◇◇◇◇◇◇◇◇◇◇◇◇◇◇◇

Contributed by Meredith Piotrow

> ½ cup vegetable oil
> ½ cup white sugar
> 1 egg
> 1 cup milk
> 2 cups flour
> 2 tsp baking powder
> a pinch of salt

Corn doesn't grow very well on the rocky, windblown summit of Mount Washington, and sometimes it's inconvenient to trudge 20 miles through a blizzard to the nearest general store. So when the Observatory crew runs low on supplies, we make due with "corn-free" cornbread.

First, preheat the oven to 425°. In a large bowl, mix vegetable oil and white sugar. Then add the egg and milk and continue to stir. Gradually stir in the dry ingredients: flour, baking powder, and salt. Stir until all ingredients are well blended, then place dough in a greased and floured 9-by-9-inch pan, and bake for 20 to 30 minutes, until firm. Serve hot.

Dinner Rolls

◇◇◇◇◇◇◇◇◇◇◇◇◇

Contributed by Mark Ross-Parent

    2 tsp active dry yeast
    white sugar (just a dash)
    ½ cup warm water
    6 cups white flour
    2 tsp salt
    1 cup warm water
    1 cup milk (skim or whole)
    2 tbsp olive oil
    4 tbsp white sugar
    1 egg white
    sesame seeds

Add yeast and a dash of white sugar to ½ cup warm water, and set aside for 5 minutes to proof the yeast. In the meantime, combine the flour with salt and also set aside.

Mix together water, milk, olive oil, and sugar in a large bowl. Then to this mixture add the yeast mixture and the flour. Mix well, until you form a ball of dough. Turn it out onto a floured board and knead for 8 to 10 minutes, adding only as much flour as necessary to keep the dough from sticking. Place dough in an oiled pan, cover, set in a warm place, and let rise for one hour, or until doubled.

Again, turn out the risen dough onto a floured board. Deflate with a rolling pin. Cut dough into 12 equal pieces and roll them into balls. Place the balls in greased muffin tins and let rise again for 40 minutes to one hour.

Preheat the oven to 350°. Combine one egg white with a dash of water, and paint mixture onto the rolls just before baking. Sprinkle the tops with sesame seeds and bake for 30 minutes, or until rolls are deep brown. Serve with butter.

Mark Ross-Parent, who worked for years as a meteorologist at the Observatory and South Pole, knows as much about bread as he does about weather. After leaving the Observatory, he went on to open a successful bakery in North Conway, New Hampshire. Whenever the aroma of baking bread wafted upstairs from the kitchen to the weather room, we knew we were in for a treat.

Blueberry Muffins
◇◇◇◇◇◇◇◇◇◇◇◇◇◇◇◇◇◇◇◇◇

Contributed by Lynne Host

For best results, hike down to the Alpine Garden, just about treeline, and pick a pailful of wild blueberries. Just be sure to leave some for the bears.

> 2 ⅔ cups flour
> ¼ cup rolled oats
> 2 ⅔ tsp baking powder
> ½ cup white sugar
> ½ cup brown sugar
> 1 beaten egg
> 1 cup milk
> 4 tbsp melted butter
> 2 cups blueberries
> 0 bears

First, sift together flour, oatmeal, baking powder, and sugars in a large bowl.

Next, add the well-beaten egg, milk, and melted butter. Stir just long enough to blend wet and dry ingredients, then fold in the blueberries—the more the merrier!

Pour the batter into greased muffin tins and bake at 425° for 25 minutes. Makes approximately 12 muffins.

Soups, Sauces, and Salads

Spring Thaw Soup
◇◇◇◇◇◇◇◇◇◇◇◇◇◇◇◇◇◇◇◇◇◇

Contributed by Kathy Trembley

This delicious soup is completely free of animal products, unless you choose to top it off with a little Parmesan cheese. Fat content is practically zero. From chopping board to serving bowls, the soup takes approximately 1 ½ hours to prepare.

> 1 lb carrots
> 2 lb yellow or white onions
> 1 bulb garlic (5 or more cloves)
> 2 cups fresh spinach
> 2 cups fresh parsley
> 2 lb tomatoes
> 1 to 2 tbsp sesame oil
> generous sprinkle of cayenne pepper (optional)

To begin, shred the carrots, slice the onions, and chop all other vegetables. Sauté garlic and onions in sesame oil (do not burn!). Add about a cup of water, and allow garlic and onions to simmer for a few minutes.

Add the rest of the vegetables, along with enough water to cover and establish a soupy texture. Cover and bring to a boil. Then reduce heat and simmer until the broth is rich and green.

If you like a little spice to your soup, sprinkle cayenne pepper in the broth. The cayenne will blend nicely if added early. Also add a dash of salt, if you like. Serving with some crusty bread that can be dipped into the soup is also a nice touch.

As is the case with many soups, this one tastes even better on the second day!

Tomato Basil Soup
◇◇◇◇◇◇◇◇◇◇◇◇◇◇◇◇◇◇◇◇◇
Contributed by Kristy Medeiors

"I made this soup for a lunch we had to prepare for the Subaru Sponsors," says summit volunteer Kristy Medeiors. "I was so nervous, knowing how much they contribute to the Observatory, I didn't want to screw up!" Fortunately, they loved it, served with tuna sandwiches and brownies. One important guest even asked for the recipe.

> 2 cans (28 oz each) crushed tomatoes
> 1 can (14 oz) chicken broth
> 20 fresh chopped basil leaves
> 1 tsp sugar
> ½ cup butter
> 1 cup whipping cream

In a saucepan, add tomatoes and broth and bring to a boil. Reduce to a simmer for 10 minutes. Add the remaining ingredients on low heat.

Rime Lemon Soup
◇◇◇◇◇◇◇◇◇◇◇◇◇◇◇◇◇◇◇◇◇

"This light, fluffy egg-lemon soup looks a little like the rime ice that covers everything on the summit," says former Observatory trustee Jill Schoof.

> 7 cans (14.5 oz each) chicken stock (equals 12 cups)
> 2 cups white rice (not precooked variety)

salt to taste
juice from 4 lemons
1 lemon, sliced very thin
8 eggs

Bring broth to a boil, then add rice and salt. Cover and simmer for 25 minutes. Remove from heat.

While the rice cooks, squeeze the juice from 4 lemons and cut a fifth lemon into thin slices.

Separate egg whites from egg yolks and beat the whites until they are stiff. Then add yolks and beat well. Continue to beat eggs while slowly pouring in the lemon juice. Next, slowly add 1 cup of hot broth to the egg mixture. Be sure to beat continuously, or else it will curdle.

Finally, blend the egg mixture into the remaining chicken broth and rice. Ladle into bowls and float a lemon slice in each bowl for decoration. Makes 12 servings.

YOU NEVER KNOW WHEN YOU'LL NEED AN
ICE SCRAPER ON MT. WASHINGTON.

Squacolli Soup

◇◇◇◇◇◇◇◇◇◇◇◇◇◇◇◇

Contributed by Dave Thurlow

> 1 butternut squash, 2 to 3 lb
> 1 large head broccoli
> 1 stick butter
> 1 lb sharp cheddar cheese (grated)
> 2 cans (12 oz each) evaporated milk
> 2 to 3 bouillon cubes (or miso to taste)
> lots of garlic and black pepper

Peel, chop, and boil the squash until soft. Be sure to save the cooking water. Chop the broccoli and steam it for just a minute or two. Melt butter and cheese in milk with the bouillon cubes or miso. Run it all through a blender, adding squash cooking water to attain the desired thickness. Season with garlic and pepper. Serve with homemade bread.

Krummholz Mushroom Soup

◇◇◇◇◇◇◇◇◇◇◇◇◇◇◇◇◇◇◇◇◇◇◇◇◇◇◇◇◇◇◇

Contributed by Jill Schoof

> 3 lb mushrooms, finely chopped
> 2 bunches green onions, finely chopped
> 4 tbsp unsalted butter
> salt and pepper
> 4 cans (14.5 oz each) chicken broth
> 2 cups water
> 1 cup dry white wine
> 2 cups whipping cream
> 4 egg yolks

Sauté the mushrooms and onions in the butter until tender, then add salt and pepper. Next, stir in the chicken broth, water, and wine. Cover and let simmer for 90 minutes.

In a separate bowl, combine the cream and the egg yolks. Add a little of the hot soup to the cream and eggs, stirring constantly. Then stir the heated cream mixture back into the soup pot, and heat to serving temperatures. Be careful not to let it boil or the soup will curdle.

Peanut Butter Soup

Former Observer Al Oxton, who went on to work in Antarctica, created (and continuously experimented with) this old summit favorite. Generally, this is a rich, creamy soup. About a cup is enough to start dinner.

> 1 medium onion, diced
> 2 to 3 cloves garlic
> olive oil
> ¾ cup peanut butter
> ¼ cup butter
> ¼ cup flour
> milk
> water or chicken broth
> a dash of black pepper
> whole peanuts for garnish

Start with a 10-inch cast iron skillet. "None of those fancy high-tech flimsy things, nor aluminum either," says Al. "The skillet must have a tight-fitting cover, too. And use wooden spoons for stirring."

Sauté the chopped onion and garlic in olive oil. After 1 or 2 minutes, add peanut butter—crunchy works best—and regular butter. ("That's real butter," insists Al. "I will not be responsible if you use any of those sickly spreads.")

Now, lower the heat and cook until all the butter and peanut butter melt and blend. Then add flour. The flour is important because it binds the fats with the yet-to-come liquids.

When the flour is all taken up by the fat, add milk. Use as much milk as necessary to adjust thickness to taste. Stir very slowly, and add milk a bit at a time. "You can also add water or chicken broth to blend the flavor one way or the other," adds Al.

"It is important to keep the whole mess moving while it is thick, so as not to scorch it. Nothing is worse than burnt peanut butter soup." Once you have adjusted the thickness to suit your taste, sprinkle on a little black pepper. Let the soup simmer for 10 minutes more, stirring occasionally.

Serve in warm bowls, and garnish with 3 roasted peanuts (still in their shells) floating on top. Crackers and a thick grape preserve work well on the side.

Creamy Garlic Sauce for Pasta
◇◇

> 2 tbsp (or more) minced garlic
> 1 onion, minced
> fresh ground pepper to taste
> 2 tbsp butter
> 1 cup light cream (use milk for a thinner sauce)
> ¾ cup grated Parmesan cheese
> ½ cup butter

Sauté garlic, onion, and pepper in 2 tbsp butter. Then add cream, Parmesan cheese, and the rest of the butter. Stir all together until sauce is smooth and hot. Pour over pasta.

Sawdust from the Log
February 23, 1992

"Nice day on the rime-covered Rockpile. Rich cooks up a fine pasta dinner. Altocumulus undulatus is sighted at the 0300 observation. Looks like troughs cut out of the fog."

Alpine Salad
◇◇◇◇◇◇◇◇◇◇◇◇◇

1 head leaf lettuce
½ head iceberg lettuce
2 to 3 tomatoes, chopped
1 cucumber, sliced
1 onion (or more), sliced and diced
2 to 3 radishes, sliced up nicely
2 carrots, thinly sliced
1 pepper, medium diced
1 can (14 oz) black olives, drained
½ jar (14 oz) pepperoncini, drained
2 small cans mandarin oranges, drained
2 tsp dill weed

Arrange vegetables neatly in a wooden salad bowl. Add black olives, pepperoncini, and mandarin oranges. Mix it all up. Finally, sprinkle the top with the secret ingredient: dill weed. Serve with a fine choice of salad dressings and chomp down.

ERIC PINDER

TIP-TOP HOUSE STANDS BEHIND THE
OBSERVATORY'S PRECIPITATION CAN.

Main Dishes

Tip-Top Tuna
◇◇◇◇◇◇◇◇◇◇◇◇◇◇◇◇
from the Blue Box

Tip-Top House, built in 1853 and gutted by fire in 1914, once offered visitors sanctuary from the winds and, sometimes, a bite to eat as well. The stonewall building that stands today is a historical re-creation, owned by the state of New Hampshire. Travelers to the summit in the 1800s might have indulged in meals like this one—not fancy, just filling.

> 1 lb (uncooked) noodles or macaroni
> 2 tbsp margarine
> 1 can peas (or 1 ten-oz pkg frozen peas, cooked)
> 2 cans condensed cream of celery soup
> 2 cans tuna (7 ½ oz each)

Boil noodles, then drain them and add margarine, tossing noodles to coat them. Meanwhile, drain the peas and add to the undiluted soup. Heat to a simmer. Drain tuna and spread over warm noodles. Pour soup over tuna. Heat over low heat (in the old days at Tip-Top House, they used to heat over a low fire), stirring occasionally for 2 to 3 minutes.

Chicken Paprikash
◇◇◇◇◇◇◇◇◇◇◇◇◇◇◇◇◇◇◇◇◇◇
Contributed by Danny Johnson

"To enhance the appreciation of this Eastern European favorite," advises longtime Mount Washington State Park ranger Danny Johnson, "whip it up after a drive through Pinkham Notch, all the while imagining you're actually on a blood-curdling journey through the Carpathian mountains, racing against the sunset. Be sure to leave the skin on the chicken so the bright orange sour cream gravy will be swirled through with the dark red grease. You can worry about your arteries later."

> vegetable oil
> butter
> 3 to 4 lb chicken (in pieces)
> 5 large onions, chopped
> 4 or more tbsp Hungarian hot paprika
> salt and pepper to taste
> 1 can (12-oz) peeled tomatoes (equals 1 pound)
> 3 cups chicken broth
> 3 to 4 tbsp flour
> 2 tbsp sweet paprika (or hot, if preferred)
> 12 oz sour cream

In a large pot or Dutch oven, brown the chicken pieces in oil and butter. Remove from pot and set aside. In the same pot, sauté onions and hot paprika until onions turn glossy red. Return chicken to pot.

Season liberally with salt and pepper. Add tomatoes and broth (enough to cover chicken). Bring to a boil. Cover, reduce heat, and simmer 1 hour, or until chicken is tender.

In a separate bowl, stir flour and sweet (or hot) paprika into the sour cream. Remove chicken to serving dish. Add some of the liquid in the pot to the sour cream mixture, then whisk this into the pot. Bring just barely to a boil, stirring. Pour over chicken and serve with egg noodles.

Chicken Cacciatore

◇◇◇◇◇◇◇◇◇◇◇◇◇◇◇◇◇◇◇◇◇◇◇

Contributed by Danny Johnson

"Skillet size is important for this recipe. Be sure to use an iron skillet big enough for an elephant to sit in and heavy enough to serve as weaponry," says Danny Johnson. "Utilizing it in either or both these manners just before confecting this crowd-pleaser adds greatly to the Old World charm of this rich meal."

    ¼ cup olive oil
    4 lb chicken, in pieces
    4 cloves garlic, minced
    1 or 2 large onions, in fat slices
    1 large green pepper, in wide strips
    2 tbsp salt
    1 tsp white pepper
    cayenne pepper (several dashes)
    ¼ tsp rosemary
    2 bay leaves
    ½ tsp thyme
    1 tsp basil
    ¼ tsp marjoram
    ½ cup Chianti or dry white wine
    1 can (28 oz) Italian peeled tomatoes
    1 can (15 oz) tomato sauce
    1 can (6 oz) tomato paste
    2 tbsp brandy
    1 cup sliced mushrooms

In a large skillet, brown chicken pieces in olive oil. Then remove chicken and set aside. Add and sauté garlic, onion, and green pepper, then return chicken to pan. Sprinkle seasonings and herbs over all. Mix together wine, tomatoes, sauce, and paste and pour over chicken pieces. Sprinkle brandy over all.

Cover and simmer one hour or until chicken is tender. Stir occasionally to prevent scorching. Add mushrooms for last 10 minutes of cooking time. Serve over pasta.

Sawdust from the Log
June 13, 1996

"Reports of raindrops the size of grapefruit! Also some rumbles of thunder and a flash or two of light. Sarah cooks up a fine spaghetti dinner. These interns will learn to cook before the end of the summer!"

July 31, 1996

"Jack and Barbara took the volunteer plunge, dishing out a perfectly palatable plate of pleasantly proportioned pizza."

Chicken and Ham Rolls
◇◇◇◇◇◇◇◇◇◇◇◇◇◇◇◇◇◇◇◇◇◇◇◇◇◇◇◇◇◇
Contributed by Lynne Host

> 4 whole chicken breasts (boneless and skinless)
> ½ cup sharp cheddar cheese, grated
> ¾ cup cooked ham, diced medium
> 6 tbsp olive oil
> ½ cup dry white wine

Pound the chicken breasts as thin and flat as possible. Top each one with equal portions of cheese and ham. Then roll it up and tie with butcher's string to form a bundle.

In a frying pan, sauté chicken pieces in olive oil until brown (usually no more than 6 minutes). Add wine, cover, and cook another 6 to 10 minutes or until tender (*not* dry).

Serves 4 normal people or one hungry mountain meteorologist.

Emil's Chicken Medallions

◇◇◇◇◇◇◇◇◇◇◇◇◇◇◇◇◇◇◇◇◇◇◇◇◇◇◇◇◇◇◇◇◇◇

Contributed by Guy Gosselin

Served cold, this dish is great picnic fare, but hot out of the oven, it makes a gourmet delight. Chicken Medallions made their debut during the thirtieth anniversary Mount Madison Volunteer Ski Patrol picnic in June 1996.

> 6 boneless chicken breast halves
> 2 tbsp minced onion
> 2 tbsp sweet red pepper
> 2 tbsp minced celery
> 1 package cream cheese (at room temperature)
> ¼ cup butter or margarine
> 2 tbsp flour
> 3 cups milk
> 2 envelopes powered chicken bouillon (or two
>   cubes)
> 1 clove garlic, minced
> juice from a ¾-inch lemon wedge
> 1 tsp grated lemon rind
> salt and pepper to taste
> dried cilantro

Also:

> pastry for a large, double-crusted pie
> about 25 toothpicks (if you use them carefully)

Pound the chicken breasts flat using a regular hammer and a small, smooth piece of plywood or board. Set aside. Sauté the minced onion, sweet red pepper, and celery in some butter, then combine with the softened cream cheese to make filling. Spread half the filling mixture over flattened chicken breasts, and roll up the breasts. Secure with toothpicks, making sure to seal the ends as best you can.

Arrange the rolled breasts on a collapsible vegetable steamer (or similar device) and lower into a covered kettle or wok to parboil (about 15 to 20 minutes). Check from time to time to make sure the filling is not leaking out. Meanwhile, roll out the pie dough.

When the chicken is firm, remove toothpicks. Cut rectangular sections of pie dough large enough to cover each rolled breast. Divide the remaining filling into six portions, spreading one portion on each of the pastry pieces. Plunk the rolled breasts down on the filling and bring the edges of the pastry dough together along the top of the breast, letting the dough overlap by about ¼ inch. Use toothpicks to secure the roll across the top. (What? You threw away the toothpicks? Well, you will need to get some more.) Leave about an inch of dough at each end of the roll. Fold and tuck the flaps for maximum closure and secure them with toothpicks as well.

Place rolls in a rectangular baking pan and bake at 350° until pastry is slightly browned, approximately 30 minutes. Refrigerate the cooked rolls.

Make the sauce by melting the ¼ cup butter (or margarine) in a saucepan. Then, with the saucepan off the fire, mix in the flour. The flour will start to thicken in the hot butter, so make sure you cream it as much as possible. Adding a little milk will stop the thickening process and make a nice, creamy mixture.

Gradually add the rest of the milk and cook over medium heat, stirring constantly until thickened. Now add the powdered bouillon and minced garlic, cooking for several more minutes over low heat. Remove from stove and add the lemon juice and grated lemon rind, stirring to blend. Add salt and pepper to taste, but watch the salt. (There may already be enough in the bouillon.) A couple shakes of cilantro will make a tasty garnish.

When the chicken rolls are well chilled, remove the toothpicks (you can throw them away now!) and slice each roll crosswise into ¼-inch medallions with a sharp knife. Lay out the medallions by overlapping them on a platter in two or three rows. Top with the sauce and serve hot (by microwaving for 4 to 5 minutes) or cold.

Serves 6 to 8 people.

Crabmeat Foo Yung

◇◇◇◇◇◇◇◇◇◇◇◇◇◇◇◇◇◇◇◇◇◇◇◇

from the Blue Box

I suppose the Observatory crew could hunt for crabs and lobster down at Lakes of the Clouds. But somehow it seems easier to buy packaged crabmeat at the store.

> 1 cup (8 oz) crabmeat
> 1 cup bean sprouts
> ½ cup onion, julienned
> ½ cup celery, finely sliced
> 3 tbsp cooking oil
> 6 eggs
> 1 tbsp soy sauce
> 1 tbsp cornstarch
> 1 tsp salt
> a dash of pepper

Put crab and bean sprouts in a large bowl and set aside. Sauté onion and celery in oil for about 5 minutes, until vegetables are limp. Then add to crab.

In a separate bowl, beat eggs. Then add soy sauce, cornstarch, and salt and pepper to taste. Pour over crabmeat and mix well. Drop tablespoons of the mixture onto a greased skillet and cook over medium heat, turning once, until brown on both sides. Repeat this step until all of the mixture is browned. Keep the crab cakes warm while making the sauce.

> SAUCE
> ½ cup water
> 2 tsp sherry
> 1 tbsp soy sauce
> 2 tsp cornstarch

Mix ingredients and cook over medium heat, stirring constantly, until thick. Then pour sauce over warm crab cakes and enjoy.

Canadian Spicy Pork Pie

◇◇◇◇◇◇◇◇◇◇◇◇◇◇◇◇◇◇◇◇◇◇◇◇◇◇◇◇◇◇◇◇◇◇

from the Blue Box

    3 lb lean pork, cubed
    2 large onions
    6 medium potatoes
    2 cups water
    2 tsp salt
    1 ½ tsp sage
    ½ tsp cinnamon
    ¼ tsp cloves
    pastry for 1 nine-inch double-crust pie

Combine pork, onions, and potatoes in salted water and bring to a boil. Let simmer for one hour and then pour off the liquid into a separate bowl. (A meteorologist in the kitchen at this moment would have to code the visibility as zero and the sky cover as VV000 due to all the "hot fog"— water vapor condensing in the cool air.) Finally, pour 1 cup of the liquid plus sage, cinnamon, and cloves back onto the meat and mix well. Serve as is, or put into pie shell and bake at 350° for approximately half an hour.

LIGHTNING STORMS ARE FREQUENT
ON MT. WASHINGTON.

Leftover Casserole
◇◇◇◇◇◇◇◇◇◇◇◇◇◇◇◇◇◇◇

This is a great way to clean out a crowded refrigerator (an important task on Tuesdays, the night before shift change at the Observatory) and use up leftover rice. For a vegetarian dish, simply omit the meat.

2 to 4 cups cooked rice (1 cup uncooked rice)
2 tbsp margarine or butter
1 small onion, finely chopped
salt and pepper to taste
2 to 3 dashes Worcestershire sauce
1 ½ cups cheddar cheese, grated
1 can (4 oz) sliced mushrooms (save the liquid)
1 cup milk
1 ½ cups diced leftover chicken, beef, or pork (or a
  combination)
1 ½ cups peas or green beans (or assorted
  vegetables)
¾ cup crushed crackers
paprika to taste

In a large cast-iron frying pan, place butter, onion, salt, pepper, Worcestershire sauce, 1 cup of the grated cheese, and the liquid from the canned mushrooms. (If you are using fresh mushrooms, use liquid from the cooked or canned vegetables.) Cook over low heat, stirring occasionally, until onion is tender and cheese is melted. Add all remaining ingredients (except paprika and cracker crumbs), placing the last ½ cup grated cheese on top.

Cover the pan loosely (leave a vent). Simmer 25 minutes. During the last 10 minutes, top with paprika and cracker crumbs. Serve directly from frying pan.

Guadalajara Night Chili

◇◇◇◇◇◇◇◇◇◇◇◇◇◇◇◇◇◇◇◇◇◇◇◇◇◇

Contributed by Guy Gosselin

Caution: This chili is not for the faint-hearted (that goes for the cook as well as the diners). Hot foods such as chili have an interesting history. Believe it or not, there is a good rationale for making food so hot that you can't taste it; the use of searing chili peppers and spices is reputed to be no more than a strategy for making "spoiled" meat edible. For people who hate to waste food, or who are trapped on a mountain with dwindling supplies, this recipe is ideal.

The cook's first responsibility is to check the refrigerator and freezer for any leftover meat that would normally be passed over. If organ meat, pork, beef, game, or chicken linger in your icebox a little past their expiration date, consider them now. Be sure to cut off any mold or "bad" meat. A long simmer will destroy bacteria and transmogrify gaminess into delicate flavor. Of course, it's fine to use fresh meat as well, if you have it.

Note: This dish requires that you start the day before!

> 1 to 2 lb dry pinto beans
> ¼ lb salt pork, cut into strips or cubes
> 1 or 2 bags (3 oz each) dry chili peppers (the hotter
>   the better)
> 1 lime, peeled
> 1 cup chicken bouillon
> 1 ½ to 3 cups water
> 4 to 6 large cloves garlic
> fresh ground pepper
> celery salt
> cumin
> 4 tbsp lard or margarine for sautéing
> 3 to 6 medium onions, slivered
> 1 sweet red pepper, sliced into 2-inch strips
> 2 lb hamburger
> 2 lb beef stew (don't trim off the fat)
> up to 2 lb salvaged meat, trimmed (don't flinch)

2 to 4 cans (28 oz each) whole tomatoes with juice
3 celery stalks
2 lb chorizo or other sausage
1 oz chili powder

Soak the beans overnight. When softened, boil them with salt pork strips until most of the fat is absorbed and beans are tender. (This usually takes about 4 hours.) Don't throw away the boiled-down liquor—you may want to use some later in the chili itself.

Also ahead of time, cut the stems and pull the loose veins out of the dried chili peppers. (Salvage the seeds and store them temporarily in a blender.) Soften the peppers in water for a couple of hours.

Make the chili sauce by combining the soaked peppers and pepper seeds in the blender with a peeled lime, chicken bouillon, water, and half of the garlic. Add fresh ground pepper, celery salt, and cumin to taste. Pureé and set aside.

Sauté onions and sweet pepper in the bottom of a 5-gallon kettle with a bit of lard or margarine. Add hamburger, beef, and salvaged meet. Fry for a while with more pepper, salt, and the rest of the garlic (minced). If you are not using any salvaged meat, add extra hamburger and/or cubed stew beef and pray this turns out okay!

After the meat is fairly well cooked, throw in the canned whole tomatoes (juice and all) and whack away at them with a sharp knife. (This may make you feel better if you've had a hard day.) Slice up the celery and throw it in. Cut the chorizo or other hot sausage into half-inch pieces and add them to the pot as well.

Next, add the beans and salt pork strips, plus as much of the chili sauce as you think wise. A blenderfull is about right, but do it a half-cup at a time and taste the results. (You want the hot chili sauce to enhance the flavor, not mask it.) You will want to add regular chili powder for body, but do it in increments and to taste. If the sauce still doesn't taste quite right, you have the liquor from the beans and pork to make adjustments. You can also add more garlic or salt and maybe some cilantro.

Let the chili simmer for at least 3 hours, stirring occasionally. Taste and make further adjustments as needed.

After all that work, this is the easiest step: Relax and have a beer or margarita. Invite your guests to taste and comment. (They can also make suggestions, but don't pay any attention.)

"By now, it is too late in the cooking process to make any fundamental changes," explains the creator of Guadalajara Night Chili, Guy Gosselin. "If, by chance, you have messed up, just smack your lips and pretend it is the best recipe you have ever made. Those who are suggestible will believe you, and will become valuable allies in convincing others. Mix more margaritas for those who persist in their disagreement, and they will eventually come around."

Serve with sopaipillas (see page 179) and warm honey (see your local beekeeper). Sweet sopaipillas make a nice complement to the chili. The hotter the chili, the more welcome the sopaipillas.

**FORMAL ATTIRE IS MANDATORY AT
THE ANNUAL GUADALAJARA NIGHT.**

Observatory Cook-Offs

The Mount Washington Observatory has a legacy of wild winds, eccentric cats (and people), and famous foods. And at no time is the culinary expertise of our meteorologists and volunteers more on display than in the summer. The State Park rangers live just a few steps away, and their presence inspires "cook-offs" with the Observatory crew.

In the Observatory logbook, one late-summer entry reads: "Plenty of ice outside, but down in the museum it's like July again—at least in terms of sales. Hundreds of hikers scramble to the summit for the weekend, and a good portion of them are folks staying for dinner. Yes, tonight is the annual Guadalajara night! Thirty-six people squeeze around three tables. After dinner, they stagger upstairs to look at the stars. Bodies scattered everywhere by night's end."

Guadalajara night was once an annual tradition, the high point and finale of the summer culinary season on Mount Washington. The tradition faded in the late 1990s. As EduTrips and overnight media visits to the Observatory became increasingly common, crowds around the dinner table became the norm rather than a special treat.

"The tradition began one night with a single pitcher of margaritas," explains the Observatory's former executive director, Guy Gosselin. "They were deemed 'the best margaritas north of Guadalajara,' and the night soon blossomed into a full-blown Mexican feast." This annual "holiday" serves up an introduction to the hot, spicy foods that will dominate Observatory meals during the upcoming winter season.

Around the Observatory dinner table, hordes of hungry meteorologists, geologists, park rangers, and invited guests sample the finest food available a mile above the sea. "The weather might be cold," says a guest, helping himself to a generous portion of spicy rice and beans, "but the food sure is hot."

Sawdust from the Blog

August 22, 2008

"I hadn't done night obs in a very long time and was ecstatic to be greeted with stars last night," writes observer Stacey Kawecki. "I was also treated to a shooting star, the color that can only come from a meteorite entering the atmosphere and burning up before reaching the ground. Tonight I think we'll be taking out the telescope and contemplating the cosmos."

August 25, 2008

"The Milky Way is clearly visible, and I saw five or six shooting stars and a few satellites," writes intern Jeff Wehrein. "All week I have been wondering what we did to deserve this beautiful clear weather. Perhaps Mother Nature is finally paying us back for the three months of fog we endured the rest of the summer."

Pizza: The Fifth Food Group

Pizza changes from day to day on top of Mount Washington. What once started as a primitive combination of bread, sauce, and cheese soon evolved into a deluxe frying-pan pizza that took hours to prepare.

To feed a normal-sized crew, we used to make four large pizzas, cooked on silver cookie pans. Then one night, after a late-evening search-and-rescue operation, the entire Lakes of the Clouds hut crew stayed unexpectedly at the Observatory for dinner. All those hungry, weary bodies wolfed down our precious pizza in just 15 minutes. To make a second, even bigger batch, we snuck upstairs and "liberated" two more trays from the State Park kitchen.

Senior Observer Norm Michaels remembers the origins of Rockpile pizza during his first stint on the mountain in the 1970s. Back then, the pizza cook du jour was a burly man named Lee Vincent.

"Lee was the transmitter supervisor for WMTW-TV on the summit," says Michaels. "The transmitter building also contained the living quarters for the TV summit crew. It was adjacent to the old Observatory and was connected to it by a covered walkway. Cooking was one of Lee's hobbies, and we often ventured over there for dinner. Though the distance was short, the wind howled in the gap between buildings, and the crossing was not always easy."

The pizza-making tradition continued in the 1990s and early 2000s, when we would still bring a few pies over to the TV-8 building every now and then. The new Observatory stands on the far side of the summit, which made the trip a rugged, rough, and unpleasant journey in bad weather. During a hurricane wind, rather than carry pizza over by hand, we could have flung it off the tower and shouted, "Catch!"

WMTW relocated its transmitter off the summit in 2002, so we said goodbye to Marty Engstrom and the rest of the TV-8 crew—our neighbors on the summit for so many decades. In February 2003, a fire destroyed the vacant TV-8 building and also the generators that provided power for the Observatory, ushering in a new era on Mount Washington. Despite the many changes over the years, pizza remains a summit favorite.

Calzones
◇◇◇◇◇◇◇◇◇

Calzones are the "pouched pizza," or sometimes the "poached pizza" if you leave leftovers in the fridge without clearly marking your name on them. At noon the next day, you may discover that someone else has already gobbled down what you had planned to have for lunch.

> DOUGH
> 1 tbsp yeast
> 1 tbsp sugar
> 2 cups water
> 2 tbsp olive oil
> 6 cups flour
> a dash of salt

Dissolve yeast and sugar in warm water, then add yeast, water, and olive oil to flour and salt. Mix together and knead dough for 5 minutes. ("You need dough?" goes the joke. "We're making pizza. Of course we knead dough!" I suppose it's funnier said aloud.)

Cut dough into five equal-sized chunks and roll flat. Let the dough sit and rise while you prepare the toppings and sauce.

SAUCE

Any tomato or pizza sauce will do. Serve the sauce warm, in a small dish on the side.

FILLINGS
1 lb mozzarella cheese
½ lb cheddar cheese
8 oz ricotta cheese (optional)
sliced mushrooms
vegetables
pepperoni or other meats

As far as toppings (or fillings) are concerned, anything goes! Each person at the dinner table gets his or her own personal calzone, so meals can be made to order. First, coarsely grate the mozzarella and cheddar, then mix together ½ cup mozzarella, ¼ cup cheddar, and ¼ cup ricotta. Repeat this step until you have as much (or as little) as you want. All other ingredients are optional and may be combined in any fashion.

For vegetarians, a spinach, mushroom, and broccoli calzone is delicious. Onions and green peppers also make good fillings. A few wild-and-crazy folks add chopped pineapple. For meat eaters, pepperoni, sausage, and hamburger are all fine choices. It helps to stir-fry the selected vegetables and meats in a pan before adding them to the calzone.

Place cheeses and fillings in the center of each pocket of dough. Fold in half and pinch the edges tightly shut so the ingredients will stay inside. Bake the calzones in a preheated 400° oven for 25 minutes, or until the dough turns light brown. Serve with a side dish of warm pizza sauce for dipping.

TOWERING SNOWDRIFTS ALONG THE AUTO
ROAD CAN MAKE PIZZA DELIVERIES TO
THE SUMMIT A BIT CHALLENGING.

Good 'n Easy Pizza
◇◇◇◇◇◇◇◇◇◇◇◇◇◇◇◇◇◇◇◇

For dinner in a hurry. If you've just walked five weary miles through the cold rain on a mountain search-and-rescue operation, the last thing you want to do is spend a lot of time preparing a fancy dinner—you want someone else to spend a lot of time doing it! But just in case that doesn't happen, here's a pizza recipe that's easy to make.

> DOUGH
> 1 package yeast
> 1 tsp sugar
> 1 cup warm water
> 1 tsp salt
> 2 tbsp olive oil
> 2 ½ cups flour

In a large bowl, dissolve yeast and sugar in warm water. Then slowly pour in the remaining dough ingredients and beat vigorously (about 20 strokes). Optional: Sprinkle a little parmesan cheese and oregano or crushed red pepper into bowl before beating. Knead dough for 5 to 10 minutes. Cover bowl and let dough rise for about 5 minutes while you prepare the sauce.

> SAUCE
> ½ cup diced onion
> 1 can (8 oz) tomato sauce
> ¼ tsp salt
> 1/8 tsp garlic powder (or one clove fresh garlic, minced)
> 1/8 tsp black pepper
> hot red pepper to taste

Mix all sauce ingredients and stir. Then return to the dough. Grease hands with vegetable oil or olive oil and spread the dough on cookie sheets. Then spread the sauce over the top.

Preheat the oven to 450°.

TOPPINGS

Sprinkle Parmesan cheese and 2 tsp oregano on top of the sauce. Then add any other toppings, such as the pepperoni or mushrooms. Finally, sprinkle the top of the pizza with 2 cups mozzarella cheese and pop it into the oven for 20 minutes. Makes one large pizza.

Gourmet Deep Dish Pizza

Be warned: This dinner takes several hours to prepare (and you'll spend almost as much time cleaning up the dishes). But the results are worth it.

Pizza and Scrabble became a tradition on my shift. On Sunday when the last EduTrip of the week departed, I'd give the week's volunteer a break and spend part of the afternoon in the kitchen. Oftentimes, I'd have to quickly wash my hands and sprint up the tower stairs with a shirt covered in flour, getting to the weather room just in time to do the "ob" (hourly weather observation). Occasionally, bad weather would force the EduTrip to stay an extra night, resulting in so many pizzas that we had to cook them in the oven in shifts. Then, at dinner time, we'd feast.

This recipe makes three gourmet pizzas.

DOUGH

We experimented with many doughs over the years, including a whole wheat dough. What works best is a variation on the Good 'n Easy Pizza dough from page 157.

Double the quantities of each dough ingredient listed there (e.g., 5 cups of flour instead of 2 ½, 2 cups of water instead of 1 cup, etc.) Also sprinkle in these ingredients:

> 1 tbsp Parmesan cheese
> 1 tbsp oregano
> a dash of crushed red pepper

In a large bowl, combine flour, Parmesan cheese, salt, oregano, and crushed red pepper. Mix together with a large fork. In a dish on the side, dissolve sugar and yeast in 1 cup warm water.

Next, add olive oil and dissolved yeast to flour mixture. Quickly pour in the extra 1 cup of warm water and mix with a spoon until all particles are moistened. On a well-floured board, knead dough for 10 to 15 minutes.

Pour a little olive oil (about 1 to 2 teaspoons) in the bottom of the original bowl, and replace the dough, turning it so that all sides are coated with the oil. Then cover bowl and let dough rise in a warm place for 1 hour while you work on the sauce.

SAUCE
5 cloves garlic
⅓ cup diced onions
½ cup mushrooms
1 tbsp olive oil

First, flatten and slice garlic. Dice onions and slice mushrooms, then sauté with olive oil in a skillet for 5 minutes.

Meanwhile, in a medium-sized pot, combine the following ingredients:

1 can (29-oz) tomato sauce
1 can (12-oz) tomato paste
2 tbsp olive oil
2 tbsp hot red pepper
1 tbsp oregano
¼ cup cheddar cheese (shredded)
¼ cup mozzarella cheese (shredded)

Stir together all ingredients except cheeses. Place pot on burner and start to cook at medium heat, stirring occasionally. After 1 minute, add the sautéed garlic/onion/mushroom mixture and stir. Add the cheeses intermittently as you cook sauce on low heat for 45 minutes. That gives you time to prepare the toppings.

TOPPINGS
1 cup grated Parmesan cheese
oregano
spinach
onions
sliced tomatoes
mushrooms
broccoli
black olives
cheddar cheese
mozzarella cheese

Any combination will work, but be sure to use generous portions of onions and mushrooms. Chopped spinach works well, as do olive slices. ("Spinach on pizza is a crime!" said one EduTripper visitor with a look of horror as he watched the dinner preparations. The taste won him over in the end, though.) Chopped broccoli heads also work, but the secret is putting them in the right place.

Now for the final step: assembling the components. Take three large cast-iron frying pans and grease the sides with olive oil. Yes, we use frying pans here on the Rockpile; this creates a deep dish pizza pie.

Split up the dough and fold into shape in each frying pan. A fairly thin dough works best; it will thicken a bit in the oven. Be sure to run the dough at least halfway up the sides of the frying pan—this is a deep pizza. If you want, pour just a little more olive oil onto the crust and roll it around so that it moistens the surface.

Once the dough is in place, sprinkle ¼ cup of Parmesan cheese on each one. Then add a dash of oregano. (Optional: If you have any leftover minced garlic, push some into the edge of the dough for extra flavor.) Only then pour on the warm sauce. Spread with a spoon. Keep the sauce thick. Next, throw on toppings: spinach, onions, mushrooms, broccoli, and olives, in that order. (Omit one or more, or add your own to taste.) Save the sliced tomatoes for later.

Next, add shredded cheese. First, sprinkle on a thin layer of mozzarella, then a layer of cheddar, then more mozzarella. Place tomato slices on top, for decoration. Sprinkle just a little more cheese on top of them, but not enough to hide the tomatoes. Add a final dash of red pepper, oregano, or parsley flakes, to taste.

In an oven preheated to 375°, bake for 45 minutes, or until cheese starts to brown.

AFTER A GOOD MEAL, SUMMIT SCRABBLE IS A FAVORITE EVENING ACTIVITY. ANY CREWMEMBER WHO MANAGES TO PLAY THE WORD 'CUMULONIMBUS' WINS BY DEFAULT.

NOAA PHOTO LIBRARY

THE WEATHER MAY BE COLD, BUT KEROSENE RICE &
BEANS (PAGE 164) HELPS KEEP THE SUMMIT CREW WARM.

Vegetarian Meals

Simple No-Crust Spinach Quiche

◇◇◇◇◇◇◇◇◇◇◇◇◇◇◇◇◇◇◇◇◇◇◇◇◇◇◇◇◇◇◇◇◇◇◇◇

1 package (16-oz) frozen spinach
1 package (8-oz) fresh mushrooms, sliced
1 ¼ cups extra sharp cheddar cheese, cut
    into ½-inch cubes
16 oz cottage cheese
3 eggs
2 tbsp flour
black pepper
paprika

First, thaw and drain the spinach, and slice the mushrooms. Cut the cheese into cubes.

Place all the ingredients in a large mixing bowl and blend with a wooden spoon. Then carefully pour the contents of the bowl into a large (9″ x 13″) glass baking dish. Sprinkle the top with black pepper and paprika. Bake at 350° for 45 minutes to one hour.

Variations of spinach quiche can be made by substituting onions, broccoli, ham, or bacon.

Kerosene Rice & Beans
◇◇◇◇◇◇◇◇◇◇◇◇◇◇◇◇◇◇◇◇◇◇◇◇

Contributed by Lynne Host

Guaranteed to warm you on the coldest winter day. When pressed, the creator of the recipe acknowledges that "two or three tablespoons of black pepper is okay, too." Adjust to taste.

One windy winter night, Lynne was cooking this meal in the Observatory kitchen while chatting away with a couple of summit co-workers. Absentmindedly, she gave the crushed red pepper a few shakes, as the recipe calls for—and then she froze. We all realized at the same instant what had happened. She had opened the wrong side of the red pepper container. Instead of a few sprinkles, a giant mound of hot red pepper now bubbled like a volcano in the skillet. Lynne shrugged—what can you do? She stirred it all in and served it an hour later.

The crew was safe. Our taste buds had long since been burned away by similarly hot meals. But the guests on the summit that night turned as red as Crayola crayons. Fortunately, only a few of them actually caught on fire.

> 1 cup brown rice
> 5 or 6 cloves garlic, crushed
> 3 tbsp olive oil
> 4 onions, sliced
> 1 or 2 green peppers, sliced
> 1 can (28 oz) crushed tomatoes
> 1 can (14 oz) shelled beans
>
> SPICES
> 19 tbsp black pepper (this is the "traditional"
>   amount, but it can be adjusted to taste. The
>   recommendation for "rookies" is 2 tbsp)
> 1 tbsp cayenne pepper
> 2 tbsp chili powder
> paprika
> crushed red pepper

Start by cooking 1 cup brown rice in 2 ½ cups of water to which you have added 2 tbsp of black pepper, one of the crushed garlic cloves, and about 1 tbsp of butter.

While the rice is simmering, heat 2 or 3 tbsp of olive oil in a large skillet and sauté the rest of the garlic. (You'll know it's ready when it smells wonderful.) Add sliced onions and green peppers and continue to sauté.

While the onions and peppers are still crisp, add the spices (the amount of crushed red pepper is left to the cook's discretion). Sauté for 2 or 3 minutes, then add tomatoes and beans. Cook until bubbly, then reduce heat. Cook an additional 15 to 20 minutes. Add water if necessary.

Finally, add hot rice and serve. Have plenty of tortilla chips, cold water, and sour cream available—and perhaps a fire extinguisher, too.

For an absolutely fiendish variation of this meal, known as *Nuclear Rice & Beans*, add ½ cup hot red pepper while sautéing the spices. Cook in a well-ventilated area.

Sawdust from the Log
November 1, 1995

"Crew gives a booming rendition of White Christmas in honor of today's modest snowfall (2.7 inches). All we need now is a fireplace and some roasting chestnuts. Nuclear beans 'n rice for dinner again tonight. No casualties this time."

Cabbage Noodle
◇◇◇◇◇◇◇◇◇◇◇◇◇◇◇◇◇◇

Contributed by Mark Ross-Parent

An old Polish dish—and an early winter favorite on Mount Washington.

> 1 cabbage, medium size
> ½ cup cider vinegar
> ½ cup water
> 1 tsp salt
> black pepper to taste
> 1 pound egg noodles
> 2 tbsp butter

Chop the cabbage into bite-sized pieces and place into a large cast-iron skillet. Add vinegar, water, salt, and black pepper. Cover skillet and simmer for 1 hour, stirring occasionally. You may need to add water at times to prevent sticking.

Cook the egg noodles al dente, then drain them, add butter, and blend them with the cabbage. Cook an additional 5 to 10 minutes and serve hot.

For an interesting variation, add one pound of cut-up Polish sausage to the cabbage while cooking.

Mushroom Stroganoff
◇◇◇◇◇◇◇◇◇◇◇◇◇◇◇◇◇◇◇◇◇◇◇◇◇◇◇

Contributed by Lynne Host

> 2 cups wide egg noodles
> 2 tbsp olive oil
> 1 lb fresh mushrooms
> 3 medium onions, chopped
> 3 cloves garlic, crushed and chopped
> 1 tsp pepper
> 1 tsp paprika
> 2 tbsp parsley

½ cup white wine
1 cup sour cream or yogurt

Cook the noodles and drain them. Meanwhile, in a large cast-iron skillet, pour in the olive oil and sauté the mushrooms, onions, garlic, and spices for 4 to 5 minutes (until just cooked). Add wine and cook for 10 minutes, stirring occasionally. Finally, add the cooked noodles and sour cream, and heat until warm.

Eggplant Parmesan
◇◇◇◇◇◇◇◇◇◇◇◇◇◇◇◇◇◇◇◇◇◇◇◇
Contributed by Helen Gerard

I've heard people say that eggplants are proof of life in outer space, because obviously these strange-looking pods don't originate on Earth. But wherever in the universe eggplants come from, they sure are delicious. Contributed by a longtime Observatory volunteer, this favorite recipe demonstrates just how good eggplant can be.

2 medium eggplants
Italian bread crumbs
6 eggs (or more), beaten
spaghetti sauce (any flavor will do)
Romano cheese
Parmesan cheese
mozzarella cheese, shredded

First, peel eggplants and slice into quarter-inch-thick slices. Dip each slice into a bowl of Italian bread crumbs, then into beaten eggs, then again into bread crumbs. (Start with a bowl of six beaten eggs for dipping; add more if necessary.)

Spray cookie sheet with cooking oil. Place eggplant slices in single rows, then spray again with cooking oil. Bake at 325° until fork-tender, approximately 45 minutes to an hour. (Rather than bake, another possibility is to fry the eggplant slices in hot oil until they turn a light golden brown. Just be sure to drain each slice between layers of plain white paper towels before going on to the next step.)

Now put a layer of spaghetti sauce in the bottom of a casserole dish. Next, add a layer of eggplant. Cover with another layer of sauce. Then sprinkle on Romano and/or Parmesan cheese. The amount of cheese can vary to taste.

Continue to alternate eggplant-sauce-cheese layers, ending with a layer of shredded mozzarella.

Bake uncovered at 325° for 30 minutes, or until bubbly.

Green Rice
◇◇◇◇◇◇◇◇◇◇◇◇
from the Blue Box

> 1 package (10-oz) frozen chopped spinach
> 2 eggs
> 2 cups milk
> ¾ cup packaged, pre-cooked rice (or 1 ½ cups
>   leftover regular rice)
> ⅓ cup onion, chopped
> 1 cup shredded American cheese
> ½ tsp garlic salt

Cook frozen spinach. In a bowl, slightly beat the eggs and add milk. Add all remaining ingredients and stir. Pour into a 10″ x 6 ½″ baking dish. Bake at 325° for 40 minutes, or until firm. Makes 4 to 6 servings.

Desserts

When a blizzard swarms over Mount Washington, no one on the summit worries much about sugar or calories. (A glance at the ingredients in some of these desserts probably tells you that much.) The crew can always work off dessert by shoveling snow or chopping ice. In fact, dessert weighs people down so that howling, hurricane-force winds don't blow them away like leaves. At least, that's a good excuse if you want to snatch the last piece of pumpkin pie.

WORKING OFF SOME CALORIES.

Pumpkin Pie
◇◇◇◇◇◇◇◇◇◇◇◇◇◇◇

Contributed by Barbara Shor

> 3 eggs
> ¾ cup brown sugar
> 2 tbsp honey
> 1 tbsp maple syrup
> ½ tsp salt
> 1 to 2 tsp ginger
> 3 to 5 tsp cinnamon
> ½ to 1 tsp nutmeg
> ½ to 1 tsp allspice or cloves
> 2 cups cooked, mashed pumpkin
> ¼ cup half-and-half or cream
> ¼ cup bourbon
> single crust for 9-inch pie

In a large bowl, lightly beat the eggs with the brown sugar, honey, and maple syrup. Add the salt and spices.

Next, stir in the pumpkin and the cream. Cream will make the custard heavier and richer than half-and-half. Add bourbon. A good, aged bourbon will make the pie smoother.

Pour the mixture into a 9″ round pie shell. (Deep pie plates work best.) Bake at 450° for 10 minutes, then reduce heat to 400° and bake for 45 to 60 minutes more. Start to test the pie at 40 minutes. When a knife poked in the middle comes out clean, the pie is done. Keep an eye on the crust—you may need to shield it from burning.

You might want to double this recipe, if you hope to have more than one slice at the dinner table—a single pie won't last long!

Yogurt Pie
◇◇◇◇◇◇◇◇◇◇◇

Contributed by Lynne Host

When you only have 4 ingredients, you know you're in for an easy-to-fix dessert.

1 container (8-oz) whipped topping
1 container (8-oz) container yogurt (any flavor)
1 graham cracker crust
fresh fruit

First, mix together topping and yogurt, and pour into a prepared graham cracker piecrust. Then put it in the freezer and chill for approximately 1 hour. Before eating, allow it to thaw for 5 to 10 minutes. Top with fresh fruit if desired. That's all there is to it!

To make the graham cracker crust:

1 package graham crackers
½ cup sugar
½ cup melted butter

Crush the crackers, then combine with sugar and melted butter. Mix well and press into a pie pan. Bake at 400° for 15 minutes.

Blueberry Streusel Cake

BATTER
3 cups flour
2 cups sugar
3 ½ tsp baking powder
½ tsp baking soda
1 dash of salt
2 cups sour cream (or yogurt)
4 eggs
2 cups blueberries

STREUSEL
¾ cup brown sugar
2 tbsp flour
3 tbsp butter
1 tsp cinnamon

ICING
2 tbsp milk
2 tbsp melted butter
½ cup confectioners' sugar (enough to make
     a loose icing)

To make the batter, sift together flour, sugar, baking powder, baking soda, and salt. Then mix in sour cream (or yogurt) and eggs. Stir well. Next, grease a large (9″ x 13″) pan and pour in the batter. Sprinkle blueberries on top.

The next step is to make the streusel. Cream together brown sugar, flour, butter, and cinnamon, then sprinkle on top of the batter (which is already in the pan). In a preheated oven, bake at 350° for half an hour.

Finally, to make the icing, mix milk, melted butter, and confectioners' sugar, and drizzle over the cake once it cools.

Mile-High Calorie Pie
◇◇◇◇◇◇◇◇◇◇◇◇◇◇◇◇◇◇◇◇◇◇◇◇◇◇◇◇◇◇◇◇
Contributed by Mike Colclough

Be warned: Simply reading the ingredients of this monster pie is enough to make you feel full.

     1 stick of butter
     1 cup flour
     1 cup chopped nuts
     1 package (8-oz) of cream cheese
     1 cup sugar
     4 oz whipped topping
     1 box instant vanilla pudding
     1 box instant chocolate pudding
     3 cups milk
     2 to 3 thin chocolate bars, broken into large pieces
     2 to 3 bananas

Cut the butter into the flour, blend in the chopped nuts, and press the mixture into a 9″ x 13″ pan. Bake at 350° for 15 minutes, then cool in the refrigerator.

Mix cream cheese, sugar, and whipped topping. When the "crust" is cooled, spread the cream cheese mixture on top.

Next, prepare the packages of instant vanilla and chocolate pudding, following the directions on the packages, except use 1 ½ cups milk instead of 2 cups. Spread the chocolate pudding in the crust and top with chocolate bars (or M&M's). Then spread the vanilla pudding on top of that. Top with sliced bananas.

Finally, spread a little more whipped topping on top of pie. Refrigerate for at least 10 minutes, or until pie thickens. Serve chilled, and start an exercise program within three days of consumption.

THE OLD OBSERVATORY WAS REPLACED BY THE SHERMAN ADAMS SUMMIT BUILDING IN THE EARLY 1980S.

His Just Desserts

Peter Crane recalls a dessert-related story from the old days, when the TV-8 building still existed. Two of the summit crew, Greg Gordon and John Howe, "were a bit set in their ways," says Peter. "Okay, stubborn." Competitive, too.

Greg had baked a cake for John's birthday. Setting the cake on the table after dinner, Greg remarked offhandedly, "You know, it's funny, but even after that big meal, I'm still so hungry I could probably eat that whole cake by myself."

John countered, "No, I don't think you could."

"He said it with such determination that Greg responded in kind," recalls Peter Crane.

"Yes I could!" said Greg.

He then proceeded to eat the entire cake, which he had so thoughtfully baked for John's birthday.

Another practical joke or "goof" involved Greg Gordon trimming off his bushy beard and Yeti-like hair, unbeknownst to the rest of the summit crew. "The change in appearance was remarkable," says Peter Crane. "He hiked back to the summit, put on sunglasses, and adopted a broken Quebec accent." His first stop was the TV building. "His longtime associate, Marty Engstrom, didn't recognize him at all. When Greg started asking for a cup of coffee in his fictionally limited English, Marty's sole word in response was 'Out!'"

Coffee Cake
◇◇◇◇◇◇◇◇◇◇◇◇

from the Blue Box

TOPPING
1 cup sugar
2 tsp cinnamon
½ cup flour
6 tbsp margarine, melted then cooled
1 ½ tsp vanilla
6 tbsp nuts

Mix together all ingredients, then set aside topping till later.

CAKE
2 eggs
1 ⅓ cups milk
3 cups sifted flour
1 cup sugar
4 tsp baking powder
1 tsp salt
6 tsp margarine, melted then cooled

First, beat the eggs and milk. Blend in sifted dry ingredients and margarine, being careful to mix only long enough to dampen all the flour. Pour into a greased 8″ x 8″ pan, then sprinkle with the topping. Bake at 350° for 35 minutes.

Pumpkin Cake
◇◇◇◇◇◇◇◇◇◇◇◇◇◇◇

4 eggs
1 cup olive oil
1 can (15 oz) pumpkin
2 cups sugar
2 cups flour
2 tsp baking powder

1 tsp baking soda
1 tbsp cinnamon
a pinch of salt

Place eggs, oil, pumpkin and 1 ½ cups sugar in a bowl. Beat together until smooth. (Use a large fork or electric mixer.)

In a separate bowl, stir together flour, baking powder, baking soda, cinnamon, salt, and the remaining ½ cup sugar. Slowly pour the flour mixture into the pumpkin mixture, stirring as you go. Blend thoroughly.

Very lightly grease a large glass baking pan (9″ x 13″) with vegetable oil. Spread batter in the pan and smooth it with a spoon. It should be about ¾ inch thick. Bake at 350° for 20 to 25 minutes. Allow to cool before serving. Add frosting if desired.

Uncle Ferd Cookies
◇◇◇◇◇◇◇◇◇◇◇◇◇◇◇◇◇◇◇◇◇◇◇◇
Contributed by Barbara Shor

If there was an actual Uncle Ferd, he had good taste. This is a wonderful crisp sugar cookie. This recipe makes a large number of cookies, but they disappear fast.

1 lb butter
3 cups sugar
4 eggs
2 tsp vanilla (or almond extract)
7 cups flour

Cream the butter and sugar until fluffy. Then beat in the eggs, one at a time. Beat in vanilla. Slowly stir in the flour, one or two cups at a time. Work in the last two cups of flour with your hands, kneading slightly. The dough should be buttery and should cling together in a mass.

Roll out the dough to a thickness of ½ inch on a lightly floured board.

Cut into shapes with cookie cutters. (If you put a little hole in the top of the cookies, they make excellent Christmas tree decorations.)

Place cookies on greased cookie sheets, one inch apart. Be careful—they spread. Brush the tops of cookies lightly with beaten egg yolk, then decorate with sprinkles or colored sugars of your choice. (Don't use chocolate chips! They don't work.)

Bake at 350° for 5 to 10 minutes, until cookies are very lightly browned at the edges. If they cook too long, they get too hard. Remove from cookie sheet immediately.

Sticky Buns

Contributed by Lynne Host

      2 packages yeast
      ½ cup sugar
      ¼ cup warm water
      3 eggs
      1 cup warm milk
      5 cups flour
      ½ cup melted butter

Dissolve yeast and a little of the sugar in warm water and set aside to proof. Beat together eggs and rest of sugar. Add milk and 1 cup of flour, and continue to beat. Add yeast mixture and another cup of flour, and beat again. Finally, add melted butter and the remaining 3 cups of flour and stir until mixed. Knead until smooth. Place the dough in a greased bowl, cover, and let rise for 2 hours.

While the dough is rising, start to prepare the "sticky" mixture:

      4 tbsp melted butter
      1 cup brown sugar
      ½ cup maple syrup
      1 cup walnuts (chopped medium)

Mix ingredients together and spread across the bottoms of two greased baking pans (9″ x 13″) to await the completed buns.

> ½ cup butter
> sugar
> cinnamon

Once the dough has risen, punch it down and divide it in half. Roll out to a thickness of ⅛ inch. Melt another ½ cup butter and brush a thin layer over the dough. Then sprinkle with sugar and cinnamon. Roll up dough and cut rolls crosswise into 1-inch slices.

Now it's time to join the sticky component to the buns. Place the rolled bun slices face down and close together in the pans, on top of the sticky mixture. Let them rise one additional hour. Then bake at 350° for 20 minutes.

Buttermilk Doughnuts

Contributed by Meredith Piotrow

> 1 egg
> ⅔ cup sugar
> 1 cup buttermilk (or use 1 cup plain yogurt)
> 2 tbsp melted butter
> 4 cups flour
> 2 tsp baking powder
> 1 tsp baking soda
> a pinch of salt
> 2 tsp cinnamon

Melt the butter, then mix all ingredients together to make a dough. Flatten dough to a thickness of ½ inch and cut into doughnut shapes.

In a heavy pot, pour enough vegetable oil for the doughnuts to float in (5 to 6 inches) and preheat it to about 375°. Fry doughnuts until brown, then flip them over until the other side is done as well.

Sopaipillas
◇◇◇◇◇◇◇◇◇◇◇◇
Contributed by Mark Ross-Parent

(Pronounced so-pie-*pee*-yahs.) Instead of dusting the sopaipillas with powdered sugar, try serving them with fresh honey.

> 4 ¼ cups white flour
> 1 ¼ tsp salt
> 3 tsp baking powder
> 3 tbsp white sugar
> 2 tbsp shortening
> 1 ¼ cups milk
> vegetable oil (for frying)
> honey

The sopaipilla is the Mexican equivalent of a doughnut or fried dough. To begin, mix together the flour, salt, baking powder, and sugar. Cut in the shortening with a fork and a knife, or use a pastry knife. Add milk and stir with a fork until a soft dough forms.

Turn out the dough onto a floured board and knead for 3 to 4 minutes. Then place the dough in a bowl, letting it sit for one hour.

Next, roll out the dough to a thickness of about ¼ inch and cut into diamond shapes. Pour 1 ½ inches of oil into a pan and heat to 375°F. Slowly add pieces of dough to the oil and turn occasionally to brown. Drain the cooked sopaipillas on paper towels and serve hot.

Rime Ice Cream
◇◇◇◇◇◇◇◇◇◇◇◇◇◇◇◇
Contributed by Ira Seskin

This wintertime camping favorite, also known as "Rockpile Crunch," tastes best with a fresh crop of Mount Washington rime ice. If none is available, plain snow will do just fine.

Caution: In the good old days when kids had to walk uphill to school both ways, all fresh snow was white and clean. Unfortunately, pollutants and acidity in the atmosphere now make it unwise to eat snow in many areas. So save this recipe for better days, when the air is clean.

> 2 quarts rime ice
> 1 can (14 oz) sweetened condensed milk
> chocolate chips
> M&M candies
> Reese's Pieces
> chopped nuts
> raisins

Place a 2-quart mixing bowl outdoors prior to a predicted snowfall (or fill it with existing rime ice). Carefully fold in the condensed milk until the mixture is slightly granular. If the milk is added too quickly, mix with a fork to correct the consistency. Fold in all the remaining ingredients until it looks and tastes right. The mixture should be soft and creamy—like soft ice cream. Use ice pellets for an extra crunchy texture.

SAYING GOODBYE TO MT. WASHINGTON,
UNTIL THE NEXT SHIFT CHANGE.

Toast out of a Toaster

On shift-change day, we were all sledding off the mountain when my co-worker, Steve, hit an icy patch. Not just any icy patch, either. Ice connoisseurs can find two very different kinds of ice on Mount Washington. Rime ice is "frozen cloud," and usually there's plenty of it on the Rockpile. Rime provides pretty good traction, making it easy to stop on a sled. Glaze, however, is dangerously slippery. Sometimes it lurks underneath the rime, surprising the unwary. Glaze is caused by freezing rain or drizzle. Steve had just encountered a hidden patch of glaze and—*whoosh*! Gravity yanked him downhill. The sled accelerated in an instant to the winter sports equivalent of Mach 2. Steve's four limbs shot out and clawed at the ground, but these "brakes" did little to slow the out-of-control sled. It swooshed over the snowdrifts, unstoppable.

Three seconds and a hundred yards later the sled smacked into a protruding boulder at the edge of the Great Gulf and stopped dead. The sled's momentum was imparted to Steve, who popped up like toast out of a toaster. He flew ten feet, arms flapping frantically, before landing in a soft bed of rime and snow at the very edge of the Great Gulf. It was a lucky escape.

The rest of us, meanwhile, had witnessed his tortuous descent. We decided to walk for a while.

About the Mount Washington Observatory

Since 1932, hardy observers have lived and worked in one of the most extreme places on Earth: the summit of Mount Washington, New Hampshire. Bitter cold, dense fog, heavy snow, and legendary wind combine to make the mountain a truly harsh place. To this day, scientists, educators, interns, and volunteers live and work on the summit of the Northeast's tallest peak, observing and documenting the "world's worst weather."

Off the mountain, cutting-edge research takes place at the Observatory's Bartlett Research Facility. In collaboration with partners such as the National Oceanic and Atmospheric Administration, National Science Foundation, University of New Hampshire, and many others, the Mount Washington Observatory conducts important research in regional air quality, mountain weather and climate, marine atmospheric chemistry, and instrument siting.

For more than a decade, Observatory outreach educators have traveled across the region in a Subaru "Weathermobile," bringing interactive weather programs into classrooms, libraries, science centers, and other locations. Observatory educators teach children and adults about the fundamentals of our weather and climate and the complex natural systems of our environment. Beginning in 2009, students across the nation will have the ability to connect with weather observers on Mount Washington through videoconferencing technology. Funded by the National Oceanic and Atmospheric Administration, the Observatory's new Distance Learning initiative will help educate students about weather and climate with the mountain's famous extremes as a captivating backdrop.

In the Observatory's Weather Discovery Center science museum in North Conway Village, New Hampshire, visitors explore unique, hands-on exhibits, which educate about the fundamentals of weather and Mount Washington's extreme conditions. Two daily "Live from the Rockpile" presentations, offered by Observatory summit staff via video conference, give museum visitors a real-time look at life on the mountain. These unique, interactive programs also help visitors understand how weather works, how weather observations are made, and what goes into the making of a forecast.

For an inside look at the Mount Washington Observatory (a 501[c]3 nonprofit organization), including current conditions, webcams, forums, and extensive weather information, as well as Observatory research and education programs, please visit **www.mountwashington.org**. Or write or call:

Mount Washington Observatory
2779 White Mountain Highway
P. O. Box 2310
North Conway NH 03860
(603) 356-2137
info@mountwashington.org

About the Author

ERIC PINDER first learned to love weather and mountains in his hometown of Cobleskill in upstate New York, where as a child he watched the stars and lunar eclipses with a toy telescope. After graduating from Hampshire College,  Pinder began his writing career with a travel essay about Maine's Baxter State Park. In the spring of 1995, he started work at the Mount Washington Observatory. As a weather observer, Pinder most often took the morning shift, waking at 4:30 to prepare the radio forecasts. He wrote three books during his time at the Observatory, and for two years edited *Windswept*, the Mount Washington Observatory's membership magazine. He also led "Understanding Mountain Weather" workshops and guided hikes for the Appalachian Mountain Club.

Pinder left the Observatory in 2002 to pursue his writing more fully. He became interested in children's literature, and his book *Cat in the Clouds*, based on the adventures of the Observatory's cat Nin, was published in May 2009 by The History Press. Pinder continues to live in Berlin, New Hampshire, and teaches Nature Writing and Writing for Children at Chester College of New England. His previous books are a first edition of *Life at the Top* (Down East Books, 1997), *Tying Down the Wind: Adventures in the Worst Weather on Earth* (Tarcher/Putnam, 2000), *North to Katahdin* (Milkwood Editions, 2005), and *Among the Clouds: Work, Wit, and Weather at the Mount Washington Observatory* (Alpine Books, 2008). Visit his web site at www.ericpinder.com.